OFFENSIVE SOCCER TACTICS

Jens Bangsbo

Birger Peitersen

Human Kinetics

Library of Congress Cataloging-in-Publication Data

Bangsbo, J. (Jens)
  [Vi angriber. English]
  Offensive soccer tactics / Jens Bangsbo and Birger Peitersen.
    p. cm.
  ISBN 0-7360-0309-6 (soft cover)
  1. Soccer--Offense. I. Peitersen, Birger. II. Title.
  GV943.9.O44B35 2004
  796.334'23--dc21
                        2003014333

ISBN: 0-7360-0309-6

Acquisitions Editor: Dean Miller
Production Editor: Melinda Graham
Assistant Editors: Scott Hawkins, Alisha Jeddeloh
Copyeditor: Barbara Walsh
Proofreader: Kathy Bennett
Graphic Designer: Nancy Rasmus
Art and Photo Manager: Dan Wendt
Cover Designer: Keith Blomberg
Photographer (cover): ©EMPICS Sports Photo Agency
Photographer (interior): pages vi, 8, 18, 40, 52, 66, 78, 90, 102, 154, and 166 ©EMPICS Sports Photo Agency; pages 30 and 112 ©Sportschrome USA
Illustrator: Mic Greenberg
Printer: United Graphics

Human Kinetics books are available at special discounts for bulk purchase. Special editions or book excerpts can also be created to specification. For details, contact the Special Sales Manager at Human Kinetics.

Printed in the United States of America
10 9 8 7 6 5 4 3 2 1

Human Kinetics
Web site: www.HumanKinetics.com

United States: Human Kinetics
P.O. Box 5076
Champaign, IL 61825-5076
800-747-4457
e-mail: humank@hkusa.com

Canada: Human Kinetics
475 Devonshire Road Unit 100
Windsor, ON N8Y 2L5
800-465-7301 (in Canada only)
e-mail: orders@hkcanada.com

Europe: Human Kinetics
107 Bradford Road
Stanningley
Leeds LS28 6AT, United Kingdom
+44 (0) 113 255 5665
e-mail: hk@hkeurope.com

Australia: Human Kinetics
57A Price Avenue
Lower Mitcham, South Australia 5062
08 8277 1555
e-mail: liaw@hkaustralia.com

New Zealand: Human Kinetics
Division of Sports Distributors NZ Ltd.
P.O. Box 300 226 Albany
North Shore City
Auckland
0064 9 448 1207
e-mail: blairc@hknewz.com

Key to Diagrams

▲ Cones

● ○ Players

⊗ Ball

∼∼∼► Path of player dribbling the ball

----► Path of player without the ball

——► Path of the ball

◖/◗ Player in given position

══► Shot on goal

◓ Floater

▲ Another set of cones

CONTENTS

Chapter 1   **Basic Rules of Possession Play**   1

Chapter 2   **Practical Training**   9

Chapter 3   **Creating Space**   19

Chapter 4   **Challenging**   31

Chapter 5   **Wall Pass**   41

Chapter 6   **Overlap**   53

Chapter 7   **Takeover**   67

Chapter 8   **Crossover and Split Runs**   79

Chapter 9   **Decoy Run**   91

Chapter 10 **Combination Drills**   103

Chapter 11 **Attacking Play: Buildup**   113

Chapter 12 **Possession: Change of Tempo**   157

Chapter 13 **Penetration and Finishing**   169

About the Authors   209

CHAPTER I

Basic Rules of Possession Play

In soccer, possession play is the way in which the players on a team deliver the ball to each other. The aim of possession play is for the team to maintain possession of the ball. Successful possession play relies on both the players' ability to pass and the players' moves to create good passing opportunities for the player in possession of the ball. The game both with and without the ball is therefore fundamental in possession play. At the same time, communication between players is a vital element in the implementation of possession play.

The Game With the Ball

A player receiving the ball should ask, "What am I to do with it?" The player must first understand the field of play; next, assess it; then make a decision; and, finally, act. This process takes place differently in individual players. The more experienced the player, the quicker she can summarize the game situation and make a decision about the action required. The amount of time a player has to think when getting the ball is often short (around 1–2 seconds), and it is therefore crucial to develop, through training, the player's ability to look up before receiving the ball and then assess whether it is more appropriate to pass or to dribble.

Dribbling

The player in possession of the ball has control of what happens next. He can take the initiative himself and create the conditions for combination play. He can also utilize the opportunities that, by their movements, his teammates create for him. Running with the ball is obviously slower than passing. There can, however, be tactical advantages to a player dribbling—for example, using it to create 2-v-1 situations, to challenge an opposing player, to create width in the game, or to set up the ball for someone else to take over. Chapters 3 and 4 deal with these tactical principles in detail. All of them require the player with the ball to be able to assess the tactical options before him and exploit them. It is important that a team have players who have the courage to take something upon themselves when the situation presents itself. This type of player is often called the creator or playmaker. Some examples of such players include Rui Costa, Michael Ballack, Claudio Reyna, and Zinedine Zidane. Through their desire to take the initiative, they create good opportunities for their teammates.

Passing

The pass is the most common action in soccer, and up to 800 passes occur during the course of a match. During the 2002 World Cup matches, for example, the Danish national team had on average 463 passes per match, of which 346 could be characterized as short passes and 117 as long passes. The World Cup champions, Brazil, had on average 398 passes, of which 297 were short and 101 were long.

To be able to pass correctly to a teammate is thus a fundamental factor in the game. A prerequisite for the pass to be successful is for the player to have mastered the necessary kicking technique. A good kicking technique, however, is no guarantee that the pass will be playable. The sign of a good pass is when it is precise, when it is at the right speed, and when it lands at the right moment. The quality of the pass can be seen in the recipient's subsequent work with the ball. A sign of the ideal combination play is that it looks untroubled. Barcelona's combination play at the beginning of the 1990s serves as an ideal to aim at.

Precision in a pass means either that the teammate takes the ball in such a way that she can immediately move with it appropriately, or that she collects it in a free space where she can move with the ball without a break of stride. The ball should be played to the player's favorite foot, or to an open space, which gives the player a suitable direction of movement. This last concept is particularly important when the receiving player has her back turned to the direction of play or is tightly marked. Players and coaches often disregard these details, but they can determine whether a team maintains possession of the ball.

If the pass is not made at the correct speed, it means that the recipient will work unnecessarily hard to be able to play the ball on. Too much power in a pass can result in the ball running away from the recipient, whereas a pass that is too weak will force the recipient to "pick up" or to leave a good position to fetch the ball and give it power with his ensuing pass. Correct power in the pass is especially important when a ball is played forward into an empty area, and in particular toward the outer reaches of the pitch.

Certain tactical combinations require a specific speed on the pass. For example, a correct wall pass must be flat and hard, so that the recipient simply needs to run on to the ball.

The timing of the pass is critical when a delivery needs to reach a fellow player while in motion. If the ball is passed too late, the opposition may have covered the dangerous area, or the teammate may run into an offside position. If the ball is passed too early, the opposition often has the advantage of their position to intercept the delivery.

The Game Without the Ball

Soccer is to a great extent a game without a ball. During Denmark's European championship matches of 1992, the Danish team was in possession of the ball for an average of 7 minutes of every half, and the total ball possession for individual players varied between 20 seconds and 3 minutes. In the Champions League tournament the ball is in play for a team an average of about 27 minutes. Juventus, as an example, had the ball in play for 23 minutes during the game against Feyenoord in October 2002. Conversely, Feyenoord had the ball in play for 26 minutes. The individual player generally touches the ball for between 1.5 and 2 minutes. The movements of the players without the ball should create good passing opportunities for the player in possession, as well as make it possible to put rehearsed combination play into action. At the same time, the movements should render the opponent's defensive work difficult. These tactical actions incorporate the attacking principles discussed in later chapters. When deciding whether to approach or distance oneself from the player with the ball in each and every attacking situation, each player must ask herself, "How best can I help the player with the ball?" Most often, it is with movement that teammates can help the player with the ball. How the teammates move depends on the game situation, but the player with the ball should preferably have the choice of both short, safe passes and long deliveries; her tactical judgment of the situation tells her which alternative to take. To run into position involves the player breaking free, so that the defending player cannot impede her when she receives the ball, as well as the player placing herself in a position that gives the player with the ball as wide a passing angle as possible.

A player can break free through a change of speed or direction. An attacking player who does this just at the point when the ball can be played has a chance of taking even a good defender by surprise. The defender's delayed reaction can be sufficient to allow the attacking player an instant's freedom in which to receive the ball (see figures 1.1 and 1.2). Against an aggressive and attentive defender, this instant will be short-lived. The pass should therefore be extremely precise and well-timed, as described earlier.

The break should also create the right position relative to the player with the ball. Placing consists of play distance and—when the player with the ball is pressured by a defender—the angle in relation to the player with the ball. This can be illustrated by an example. In figure 1.3, player 1, in black, has the ball and is under attack from white player 11. The only member of the team who can be played is black 2. But black 2 is so close to black 1 that he will immediately come under pressure from white 11 and 9 if he gets the ball. He risks losing the ball or could be forced to kick it up the

Figure 1.1 Defender's delayed reaction.

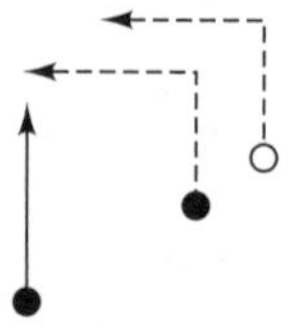

Figure 1.2 Attacking player receives ball.

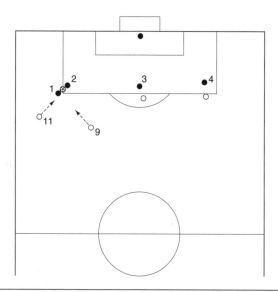

Figure 1.3 Player 1 under attack.

pitch. In figure 1.4, black 2 has taken up a position that will give him more time to work with the ball when it comes to him. The distance between the players should be adapted by black 2 so that neither the passing player nor the player receiving the ball encounters any difficulties in passing and receiving. As can be seen from figure 1.5, black 2 should move out of the passing shadow (the area behind the defender lined by his physical effort to hinder a forward pass) so that black 1, who is pressured by white's player, can pass to him. Player 2 should move at

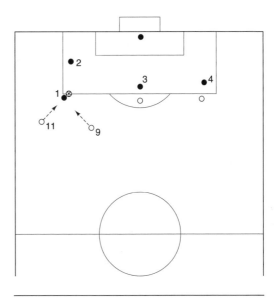

Figure 1.4 Player 2 in a position to receive the ball.

right angles to the shadow border; that is, a bit diagonally forward, so that black 1 gets a passing angle of about 45 degrees. Ideally, possession play is forward-looking, but the player with the ball should also be assured of passing opportunities behind him, especially when he is under pressure in

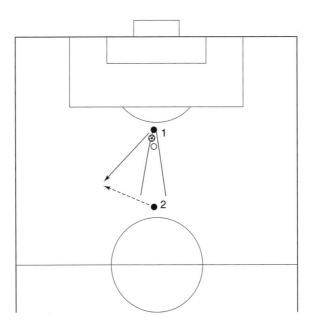

Figure 1.5 Black 2 moves out of the area behind the defender to be in a good receiving position.

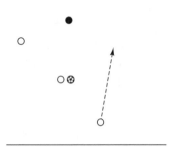

Figure 1.6 Supporting player moves ahead of player with the ball.

front from a defender. The supporting player will have the advantage over the player with the ball in that, on receiving the ball, he will have a wider passing angle in front of him. The supporting player can go ahead of the player with the ball when he is not under pressure or is about to be pressured. In figure 1.6 we see an example of this. Italian teams often use effective supporting play; they maintain back-passing possibilities even in the most pressured situations.

A player who breaks toward the player in possession of the ball creates the basis for short, safe passes. Furthermore, she wants, through a possible pass, to come into contact with the ball at a timely moment. By meeting the ball actively, the player receiving the ball can decide upon a new direction of play either by her control or through turning, both of which should prevent the defender from tackling.

Breaking away from the player with the ball creates the conditions for depth in the game, and for bringing the ball forward quickly on the pitch. A player breaks away from the player with the ball to find areas into which the ball can be passed or to create free space that other players can exploit. The player should move in such a way that he can see the path of the ball, and on receiving the ball can be in a position to see as much of the area of play as possible. In figure 1.7 the player runs across the line of the ball. He can see the line that the ball is likely to take, and he also has the whole playing area in front of him when he receives the ball.

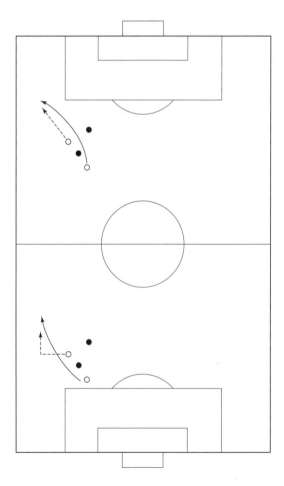

Figure 1.7 Player runs across line of ball.

In general, therefore, the player who wants to receive a pass should focus on her movements relative to the ball, how her first contact with the ball will occur, and her direct movement with the ball in the ensuing play. The aim in receiving a pass is for the recipient to quickly and safely get into a position facing the direction of attack, and simultaneously be able to play or dribble past her marker.

It is difficult for a player to receive a pass with his back turned to the direction of play. Playing the ball forward to a tightly marked attacker, however, can be exploited tactically. It is a situation that occurs often in English, Italian, and Spanish soccer. In England the ball is played from the back row directly to the so-called target player, who is the front attacker. His task is to be able to direct the ball onward to forward-running midfielders. In Italian and Spanish soccer the recipient comes quickly forward to the ball and shields it by turning sideways onto the closely covering defender. By keeping hold of the ball, even when the marking is physically close, the player is aiming either to provoke a free kick or to allow other players to get into good positions. Among British players, Alan Shearer of Newcastle is a good example of someone who can retain the ball in tight marking situations, while Italy's Christian Vieri and Patrick Kluivert of Barcelona best illustrate the Latin version.

Communication

Communication between the player with the ball and her teammates plays a vital part in creating good possession play. It can take many forms: shouts or calls; gesticulations, such as pointing; eye contact; or movement. The more attempts at communication the teammates make, the better the situation will be for the player with the ball. Players who talk a lot together about passing opportunities, about the movements of the opposition, and so forth contribute greatly to the establishment of good possession play. A team can learn communication via training and matches.

A mutual understanding of passing situations between the players creates a good network for beautiful and effective combination play. When Ronaldo made his 2002 entry on the Real Madrid side, his first appearances gave an example of the way in which a pass is good only if two players read and interpret a playing situation in the same way. Ronaldo's passing work with Raul, in particular, was often—too often—futile. Passing collaboration is like a language. When, for example, Ronaldo puts a gentle pass in to Raul, he is trying to tell Raul to meet the ball actively as he has a defender close behind him. But if Raul does not understand the language, then problems arise in reading the game. Those who wish to learn a language (the language of soccer) must learn the grammar, and they must practice. They must do this both alone and with those with whom they wish to speak (i.e., play).

CHAPTER 2

Practical Training

This chapter outlines general and specific considerations the coach should make when planning tactical training. Concrete advice is provided about the ways in which training sessions can be carried out. The chapter ends with an overview of the way in which this book describes the individual tactical attacking principles.

Planning

Before the season begins, the coach should consider, taking into account his soccer philosophy and player resources, what he wants the team and its players to achieve within the tactical arena during the course of the season. Once the objectives have been set, the coach must develop a long-term plan to fulfill those objectives.

The long-term plan must not be seen as an immutable entity. Many teams can change their plans en route to achieving their goals. As a consequence of the team's or individual players' mistakes in matches, the coach may need to reprioritize the main objectives for a while to set the team and players back on the right track. On occasion, the team's work toward the main objectives reveals new opportunities for development, which may cause the coach to consider revising these objectives. Players can develop differently than anticipated, so there may be grounds for adjusting the long-term plan.

When planning the tactical training, the coach should always consider the players' technical, physical, and psychological levels, because these can determine how profitable the training actually is. What good is it, for example, if the attacking players know and understand how to use the crossover run but are not quick enough to sprint away from the markers (physical shortcomings)? What is achieved when the team is continuously in a position to create overlap situations along the sidelines but none of the players can kick the ball into the center of the field (technical shortcomings)? What is the benefit of a player exploiting a free space if, despite good technical preparation, he cannot score from free positions (psychological problems)?

For the purposes of this chapter we will assume that the coach has chosen a certain attacking tactical area as the subject for training.

Organization

Once the coach has assessed what she wants to work on and has selected drills, she should consider how the training session is to be organized. She should know in advance where on the pitch the drills will take place and how to make the transition from one drill to the next. The coach should also plan which and how many pieces of equipment will be used. If it is obvious beforehand that a part of the training time will be needed to complete preparation for new drills, the coach should consider, before the training session, what the players should do on their own while they are waiting. Tactical training is often related to specific player positions and formations. The coach should thus think ahead of time about which players should work together in training groups.

In practice, a coach frequently does not know in advance how many players will be attending the training session. It is therefore important that he has considered before training what to do if there are fewer, or occasionally more, players than he had planned for. Regardless of how much thought the coach has put into a training session in advance, however, unexpected situations will arise. The likelihood of being able to handle even these situations increases if the coach makes a habit of thinking through different potential problems.

Carrying Out the Training

While the session is taking place, it is important for the coach to constantly ask himself, "Are the players doing what I want them to?" Or, put another way, "Is the practice fulfilling the requirements I have made of it?" If the answer to these questions is no, the coach should intervene. This intervention can consist of simply additional guidance, whereby the players achieve a better understanding of how to apply the principles of the drill. Sometimes the coach is forced to change the drill, for example, to introduce new or remove existing rules. Occasionally, drills are carried out that look good on paper but do not work when put into action. If the coach sees no immediate possibility of improvement, the drill should be stopped. Subsequently the coach can revert to the drawing board to decide whether the drill can be made useful; if not, it must be rejected. Players often go through a period of adjustment before a drill produces the desired effect. If the coach uses a drill repeatedly over longer periods, it is appropriate to evaluate and fine-tune it as an ongoing process. This is because, among other things, part of the drill's effectiveness relies on the players' tactical and technical levels. A drill that works well for one group of players will not necessarily be satisfactory for another. The choice of instruction method and form of training depend on the goals for the training session, the age of the players, and the stage they are at in terms of soccer development. The following section provides some general principles as well as advice on instruction and guidance.

Preparation

The coach should

- Be thoroughly familiar with all the drills and know the exact order in which she wishes to run them, so that she does not need to stand with papers in hand during the instruction. She can leave her schedule in a pocket and consult it while the players are carrying out the drills.
- Be clear in her mind as to how much instruction and guidance she wants to give in a drill.

Starting Off the Training Session

The coach should

- Summarize at the start of a training day the aims of the session and outline what is to happen during the course of the session. The coach should avoid going into too much depth, because the players will have difficulty remembering all the details.

- Avoid long explanations before the drills; he should preferably demonstrate the practices in the playing area after the players have taken their positions. It can sometimes be advantageous to have players start the drills without special comments and save the in-depth explanations until the players have become accustomed to the playing area.

Execution of the Drill

The coach should

- Focus the instruction and corrections on what she wants to train (i.e., the aim of the session), making additional comments only to facilitate the flow of play.
- Avoid interrupting the drill too often to gather the players together for further instruction; frequently the guidance can be given during a brief pause in the playing area.
- Get the players accustomed to stopping short at a given signal. After a brief pause for thought, guide the players using the chosen principle as a basis. Following the instruction the players can carry out the corrected moves and passes in such a way that they can see and understand the benefit of correct action. Play should also be stopped when a player performs the desired action successfully, especially if it is a player the coach has recently corrected.
- If playing with rules and points or goals, ensure that the rules are upheld and that score is kept for the points or goals. Points and goals can often be used for motivation, especially toward the end of a practice. It is, however, a good idea to get the players themselves used to judging and keeping score within their positions.
- Limit the use of a whistle, which can otherwise be perceived exclusively as a function of a referee.

Positioning the Players

The coach should

- When the players are gathered in for instruction, stand facing them at a suitable distance. The balls should be together in such a way that the players don't lose concentration by playing with them. Likewise, the players should not, where possible, be able to look at anything nearby that could distract their attention, such as a soccer match. During longer explanations it is sometimes better to sit the players down, weather conditions allowing.
- When demonstrating a practice with some of the players, make sure that the rest are positioned at a distance where all can see what is going on. The coach should also avoid talking into the wind and should make sure the players do not have the sun in their eyes.

- During the drills, avoid turning his back to the players as much as possible while observing them. The coach should remain at a good distance from the players, but not so far away that he cannot intervene quickly where necessary.

Behavior and Voice

The coach should

- Avoid chatting and talking constantly, so that the players really listen when she speaks.
- Speak with a loud, clear voice when she instructs and guides.
- Show involvement. The players should have the impression that the coach is very much engaged in high quality training.

Finishing the Session

The coach should:

- After a drill or training session, outline the main ideas that were introduced, possibly by reconstructing one of the situations that occurred during the session.
- In closing, inform players of the coming session's key points.

Format of the Attacking and Tactical Principles

Chapters 3 through 9 describe different attacking principles and tactical principles, respectively, within attacking play. Each principle is presented according to a certain format. This section lists the headings you will find in those chapters and briefly summarizes how the principles are presented, the intentions of the different elements, and how to carry out the drills on the pitch.

- **Principle.** The principle is outlined in simple phrases.
- **Usage.** Game situations into which the principle can be incorporated are described.
- **Aims.** Concrete training objectives with regard to the principle are provided. These can in certain cases include other principles too.
- **General Description and Hints for Instruction.** The main section lists a range of points and subpoints that detail the most important characteristics of the principle. In addition, we have noted some

particular things the coach should watch for when the players are practicing the principle.

Within each principle, we have provided a number of drills that can give players the opportunity to practice each principle. There are two main categories of drills: illustrative and performance.

Illustrative Drills

For each principle, both illustrative and performance drills are included. In the illustrative drills the movements are preset. For the performance drills the players have greater freedom of movement, though their actions are still limited.

The object of the illustrative drills is to introduce the principle to the players and help them understand the way it can be used within a game. For this reason the drills are carried out on a large pitch. It is important that the coach be painstakingly exact during instruction of these drills. It can be appropriate to introduce the players to certain keywords, which both coach and players can subsequently use in performance drills and during actual match situations.

The first time the team carries out an illustrative drill, all players can try out the different roles. Later on the drill can be executed using those players who are most likely to make use of the principle in match play.

Several factors are common to all illustrative drills:

- The defenders on the field should be comparatively passive at first, but in the penalty area they should perform with maximum activity. When the players have tried the drill a number of times, the defenders can be fully active at all times; however, they should not exploit their knowledge of the drill to take up a proper defensive position beforehand. Once the players are familiar with the variations provided within each drill, this last condition can be disregarded.

- A drill is completed by scoring, either when the ball is played out of the penalty area, or when the goalkeeper has control of the ball. If the defenders win the ball outside the penalty area, the attack is finished once two defenders have touched the ball consecutively.

- A player serving the ball to an attacker should move into the penalty area and join in the ensuing attack.

- Carry out the illustrative drills with several groups of players. This will allow each group sufficiently long breaks between repetitions of the drill so that when it is their turn they are able to work at a high level of intensity.

Most of the drills can be carried out simultaneously on both halves of the pitch. The groups can switch ends after completing each repetition. So that everyone may try out the different roles, have the players rotate one place every other time the drill has been completed.

Performance Drills

It is possible to train a principle in a match-like situation by requiring the use of a principle to score, or by awarding points for correct performance. Such conditions often make the drills artificial and the execution of the desired principle inexpedient. In the performance drills described in these chapters, the players should practice each pertinent principle in a more or less natural manner. The special conditions inherent in the drills make it beneficial to the team to make use of the relevant principle.

Specific Warm-Up Drills

At the end of each chapter you will find a range of warm-up drills that can be used as preparation for practicing that chapter's specific principle. The warm-up drills give the players an idea of what the relevant principle is about. The drills can also be used after the players have practiced the principle to reinforce what they have learned. For a key to diagrams, see page 16.

General Drill Description

Each drill will contain some or all of the following headings.

Pitch

An approximate pitch size is suggested.

Players

The number of players is adapted to the size of the pitch. If you have fewer or more players than indicated in the drill, it may be necessary to narrow or widen the playing area accordingly.

Special conditions

Any special preparations required to set the drill in motion are outlined here.

Description

Simple phrases describe what happens in the drill. "Normal play" means the players follow the rules of soccer, although they do not use the offside rule.

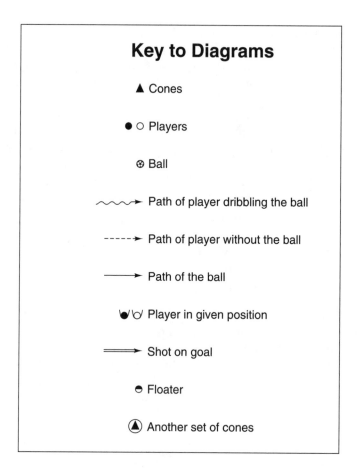

Key to Diagrams

▲ Cones

● ○ Players

⊗ Ball

〜〜➤ Path of player dribbling the ball

----➤ Path of player without the ball

——➤ Path of the ball

◖/◗ Player in given position

⟹ Shot on goal

⊖ Floater

▲ Another set of cones

Special rules

Any rules other than normal play used in this practice are described here.

Scoring

The form of scoring is, as a rule, adapted to fit the aim of the drill, but on some occasions the method of scoring can be altered without the drill losing any of its effectiveness.

Variations

The drills offer several developmental possibilities; this section suggests ways to extend work with the drill. In the performance drills, some variations are suggested that can be used independently of one another. The coach can introduce the variations to focus on other aspects of the relevant principle, or simply for a change of pace.

Hints for instruction

Here we define the object of the drill and describe what the coach should focus on during its performance. We also denote the anticipated effect that introducing one of the developmental variations will produce.

Keywords

For every drill we have provided keywords that may profitably be incorporated into the training session. Through this, players and coach develop a common language, which simplifies the coach's task of directing the players. Detailed descriptions of the relevant keywords are found in the "General Description and Hints for Instruction" section.

CHAPTER 3

Creating Space

Creating space is an essential purpose of an attack. In all other attacking principles as they are presented in chapter 4 to chapter 10, the basic principle comes back to players' ability to create and exploit free space on the field.

Principle

A player creates space through his movement for either himself or a teammate to exploit (see figure 3.1).

On receiving the ball, the individual player should create space for himself so he can keep hold of the ball. In this chapter, however, we concentrate solely on the team tactic of creating and exploiting free space.

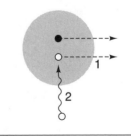

Figure 3.1 Player 1 creates space for player 2.

Usage

With 22 players spread out on a pitch of about 102 by 65 meters, despite the limits set by the offside rule, spaces exist that are or can become free; that is, where no opponent is in the immediate vicinity. For an attacking team it is vital to create and exploit free spaces to obtain varied and effective possession play. This can happen individually, in pairs, or as a team. Figure 3.2 shows an example of the way in which a midfielder creates space for a fullback.

The vast majority of runs in soccer are made by players not in direct contact with the ball. For example, analyses of the Danish players during the 1992 European Championships showed that the players had possession of the ball for an average of one minute each during a match, ranging from 20 seconds to three minutes. As they practice creating and exploiting free space, the players should become aware that through their runs, they can help other team members find more space. The coach should regularly point out the importance of running without the ball. The players will often need encouragement, because players and the public often misunderstand and undervalue these runs. One often hears players say, "I'm not bothering to run in position any longer, because I never get the ball." These players should be made to understand that through their own movements they can create space for others. The training can motivate them to continue and possibly increase the number of such often-effective runs.

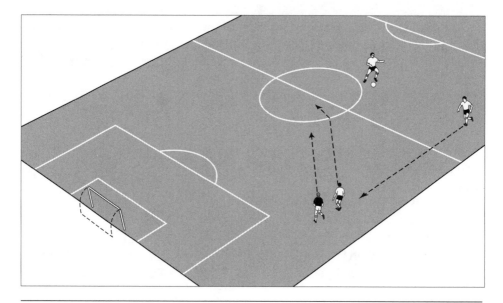

Figure 3.2 Midfielder creates space for fullback.

Aims

1. To give oneself or one's teammates an opportunity to receive the ball in an area where there are few opponents
2. To give the player with the ball more space in which to maneuver

General Description and Hints for Instruction

The creation and exploitation of free space is inherent in all attacking tactical maneuvers, and it is therefore extremely important that the players understand the principle. The coach and players should pay particular attention to this concept in that it is fundamental to all other attacking principles.

Main Point for the Player Creating Space

Running speed

Using movement, an attacker creates a free area by luring a defender to follow her. She can accomplish this by running at a moderate speed; she must not run so slowly as to give the defender time to read the situation.

Main Point for the Player Using the Space

Change of tempo

It is often necessary for a player to run at high speed into the free area to make use of it.

Main Points for the Player With the Ball

Assessment

The player with the ball should assess whether to pass it to the player in the free space.

Timing of the pass

A pass should fall at the moment that the player who is using the space can run onto the ball and exploit his speed. If this does not happen, the player risks closing the gap before he receives the pass.

Drills for Creating Space

Approach Run

Figure 3.3 Approach run.

Pitch

About one-third of the pitch and a full-size goal

Players

5—one striker (10), one midfielder (7), and one fullback (2); one defender (5), who marks 10, plus a goalkeeper (1)

Description

Player 2 passes to 10, who plays 7. 10 runs across and 7 passes to 2, who dribbles to the goal line and plays the ball inside to either 7 or 10 (see figure 3.3).

Scoring

As normal

Variations

1. Add another defender (6), who is positioned between 7 and 10.
2. 10 does not have to pass to 7, and 5 does not need to follow 10 across the pitch. 7 can choose to play to either 2 or 10.

Hints for instruction

In the first part of the drill, 10 should understand what is required to create space for 2. Player 7 should get an idea of when it is appropriate to pass to 2. It is important at the beginning that 10 run across, partly to get the marking player away and partly to avoid running into an offside position.

In variations 1 and 2 greater demands are made of 7 and 10 to be aware of where the space is. Give the players a long break between performances of the drill so that they can maintain a high intensity while practicing. The drill can be carried out with four teams who alternate (two from each side of the pitch). When one team has finished the drill, a team from the other side starts their approach, and so on.

Keywords

The player creating space: running speed

The player using space: change of tempo

The player with the ball: assessment; timing of the pass

Runs From the Back

Pitch

Half the pitch and one full-size goal

Players

9—two strikers (10 and 11), one midfielder (6), and two fullbacks (2 and 5); three defenders (3, 4, and 7), of whom two (3 and 4) are marking 10 and 11, plus one goalkeeper (1)

Figure 3.4 Runs from the back.

Description

The attacking team pass to each other until one of the strikers (10 or 11) creates an open space for 2 or 5 by their running, at which time the ball is played into the open space. After this 2 (or 5) dribbles to the goal line and plays the ball inward to either 5 (2), 6, 10, or 11 (see figure 3.4).

Special rule

The offside rule is in force.

Scoring

As normal

Variations

1. 2 and 5 may also receive the ball in the middle behind 7.
2. The marking defenders are not forced to follow 10 and 11.

3. Add one extra defender. Free play (no restrictions). The defending team scores if the player who wins the ball can play it into the center circle with a high ball (no other defenders may touch the ball).

Hints for instruction

One of the aims of the drill is to get the fullbacks accustomed to keeping an eye on what the strikers are up to, and to give them an understanding of how and when free space can be exploited. The midfielder should get an idea of when it is most appropriate to pass to exploit the free space. The strikers should be aware that with their movements, they can create free space for players coming from behind.

Variations 1 and 2 increase the players' need to orient themselves. In addition, the strikers will get a feel for how their runs can risk closing off the free space for their teammates.

In variations 2 and 3 the strikers should gain an understanding of the factors that determine whether they or their teammates become playable. For example, 11 can run toward 5 (decoy run) when 5 has the ball, then 10 can exploit the space created by 11. If the player marking 10 does not keep up, 10 can be played in a free position; if not, there is free space for 2.

Keywords

Player creating space: running speed

Player using space: change of tempo

Player with the ball: assessment; timing of the pass

Making Space

Pitch

About a third of the pitch; a full-size goal and a small goal (see figure 3.5)

Players

8—four attackers (6, 7, 10, 11), three defenders, and one goalkeeper

Description

Normal play

Special rule

Two of the attackers (6 and 7) can score only within the 11-meter area, which makes up the penalty area (scoring restriction).

Scoring

The attackers score in the full-size goal and the defenders in a small goal in the middle of the field.

Variations

1. The offside rule is in effect for the attackers.

2. Add an extra attacker and defender into the drill.

3. Introduce one extra defender.

Hints for instruction

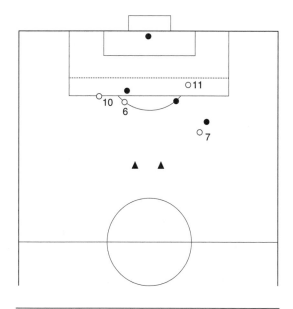

Figure 3.5 Making space.

The defenders will focus attention on 10 and 11, who by their movements can create open space for 6 and 7.

In variation 1 players can focus particular attention on the timing between pass and movement in the open space. In variation 2 the coach should urge the attackers to play the ball wide to get the defenders to move away from the center. Variation 3 increases the demands on the strikers. They should work at a high level of intensity while timing their movements to correspond with each other.

Keywords

Player creating space: running speed

Player using space: change of tempo

Player with the ball: assessment; timing of the pass

Keyhole

Pitch

Half the pitch, with marked free areas (see example in figure 3.6); two full-size goals

Players

14—6-v-6, plus one goal-keeper on each team

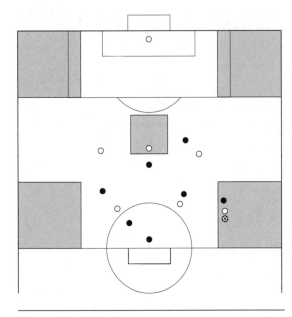

Description

Normal play

Special rules

No more than one player from each team can be positioned in one of the marked areas at one time. Also, the defending team is allowed a player in an area only if the team in possession of the ball has a player there.

Scoring

As normal

Figure 3.6 Keyhole.

Variations

1. After touching the ball in one of the marked areas, a player must leave that area.
2. The players work in pairs within the team. A pair can use only the open space in the middle or the free areas on one of the wings.

Hints for instruction

The drill focuses on the general principles for creating and exploiting space. A player in one of the free areas should consider when it is appropriate to leave the area to allow another team member, such as the player in possession of the ball, to use the space.

In variation 1 the players are forced to run away from the open spaces, which creates an area of space for another team member to exploit. In variation 2 two players, such as a right back and a right midfielder, can develop teamwork. It can be appropriate to introduce more players.

Keywords

Player creating space: running speed

Player using space: change of tempo

Player with the ball: assessment; timing of the pass

Moving Zones

Pitch

About half the pitch, divided into four zones lengthwise— two wide zones (1 and 4) and two central zones (2 and 3); see figure 3.7

Players

16—8-v-8

Description

Normal play

Special rules

A team can have no more than three players in any one zone.

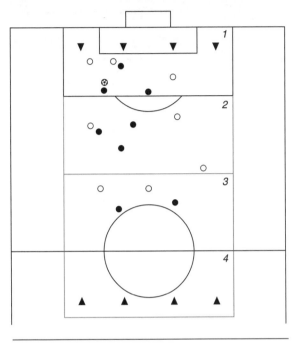

Figure 3.7   Moving zones.

Scoring

A team scores points by hitting one of the four cones in the opposition's defensive zone (1 or 4).

Variations

1. No more than two players from each team can be in zones 1 and 4, and no more than three from each team in zones 2 and 3.

2. No more than three players from each team can be in zones 1 and 4, and no more than two from each team in zones 2 and 3.

Hints for instruction

In addition to the general principles of creating and using space, this game focuses on players being able to orient themselves relative to teammates. It also encourages the players to think about how they can use their movements to create space for teammates. Variations 1 and 2 increase still further the need for orientation.

Keywords

Player creating space: running speed

Player exploiting space: change of tempo

Player with the ball: assessment; timing of the pass

Specific Warm-Up Drills for Creating and Exploiting Free Space

Continuous Passing

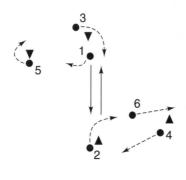

Figure 3.8 Continuous passing.

Pitch

Place two cones approximately 15 meters apart, each with another cone placed about 5 meters from it

Players

6

Description

2 runs toward 1, who plays 2, who with her first touch passes to 3, who with one touch passes to 4, and so on. After passing, a player should run around a cone and then back to receive another pass (see figure 3.8).

In and Out Passing

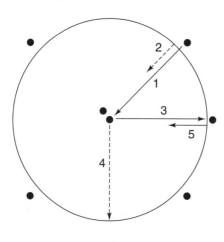

Figure 3.9 In and out passing.

Pitch

Area equivalent to the center circle

Players

7

Description

Two players start in the center of the circle while the rest are around the periphery of the circle. A player in the peripheral zone passes to one of the players in the middle and runs into the center. The player who receives the ball passes to a player in the periphery and moves toward a space in the periphery (see figure 3.9). All passes should be taken first time, as much as possible.

Chasing Challenge

Pitch

Half the penalty area, divided into four zones

Players

4—three attackers (1, 2, and 3) and one player chasing the ball (4)

Description

The three attackers must each be in separate zones. The two players who do not have the ball must be in the zones closest to the ball (see figure 3.10). Each player has a maximum of three touches. The chasing player must try to touch the ball and, if he succeeds, the attacker who loses the ball becomes the chasing player. To motivate the players, institute a rule that 10 passes without ball contact by the chasing player will give the chasing player an extra turn. After the ball has been won, allow players to take a short break so they can maintain a high level of intensity during the drill.

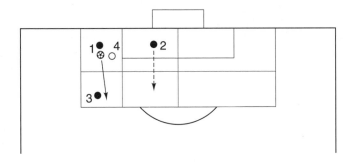

Figure 3.10   Chasing challenge.

CHAPTER 4

Challenging

The outcome of a 1-v-1 situation in a soccer match often determines the game's result. It is therefore vital that players have the courage to challenge an opponent, even though this is a risky action. If the individual players on a team simply pass the ball on without an attempt to challenge the opponent, this is called "alibi" soccer.

Principle

A player dribbles toward an opponent to force her to defend actively and thereby creates space (see figure 4.1).

Usage

Aside from the purpose of dribbling past an opponent, a challenge may be used to direct the opponent's attention, thereby creating open space for other members of the team.

Figure 4.1 Player creates space.

Figure 4.2 Passing maneuver.

Figure 4.2 demonstrates a Zinedine Zidane specialty, where he lures an opponent away from an area that he then utilizes by passing to a fellow player who has broken free.

Challenge situations also have a psychological aspect. By dribbling directly toward a defender the attacking player shows strength and self-confidence, which can make the defender uncertain and hesitant.

Most teams have certain players with a capacity for dribbling that makes it natural for them to challenge a defender in situations where they may create either an advantageous 2-v-1 situation or a breakthrough and finish. Many memorable examples of the art of dribbling were noted in the most recent European Championship and World Cup tournaments, displayed by, among others, Ronaldo, Figo, Toti, and Zidane.

Aims

1. To beat a direct opponent and thus create a situation where your team is superior in numbers
2. To utilize free space
3. To create free space for other members of the team
4. To demonstrate psychological resources (courage)

General Description and Hints for Instruction

Main Points for the Challenging Player

Assessment

The player should assess when it is appropriate to challenge an opponent. The challenge has the best chance of succeeding if the defenders are badly organized in the area where the ball is, and if the nearest defender is moving forward. If the attacker is moving at a good speed when he receives the ball, he has a good chance of beating the opponent.

Courage

The dribbling player must show courage to dribble directly toward an opponent.

Change of tempo

After challenging, the player must increase his running speed to slip past the opponent or to lure the opponent to move with him.

Main Points for Other Members of the Team

Move away/become available

Teammates in the area of play must consider how best they can help the player with the ball in the particular situation. Some should look to run out to create space for the dribbling player, and others should run toward the player with the ball to make themselves available, thus forcing the defenders to watch them all. One or two players can make themselves available in the open space created by the challenging player.

Two Against One

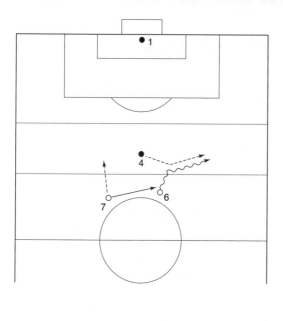

Figure 4.3 Two against one.

Pitch

About half the pitch, with a central zone and a full-size goal

Players

4—two midfielders (6 and 7), a defender (4), and a goalkeeper (1)

Description

7 and 6 pass to each other while moving toward 4, who is restricted to the central zone. The ball should be dribbled into the central zone. The player who dribbles into the central zone must challenge 4 (see figure 4.3). The offside rule is in force.

Variations

1. 4 may close in on 6 and 7 outside the central zone.
2. Introduce another defender (5) and another attacker (11). When a defender is beaten free play is established.

Scoring

Normal

Hints for instruction

This drill emphasizes the general demands on the challenging player and her teammates. 6 or 7 should challenge 4 and try either to dribble directly on goal or to take 4 with her, creating that space for a pass to her teammate. The two attackers can vary when and how they enter the zone. 4 may be given information as to which side she must defend to force 6 and 7 out in certain situations.

In variation 1, 6 and 7 are forced to evaluate 4's defensive technique immediately. Variation 2 increases the demands on the players with regard to awareness.

Keywords

Challenging player: assessment, courage, change of tempo

Other members of the team: move away/become available

Three Against Three

Pitch

About a quarter of the pitch, with an extended penalty box (see figure 4.4)

Players

6—3-v-3

Description

Normal play

Scoring

Players score points by dribbling over the opponent's goal line with the ball under control.

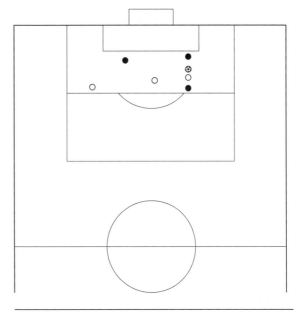

Figure 4.4 Three against three.

Variations

1. Players take a minimum of five touches each time they come into contact with the ball in the opposition's half of the field.
2. The ball may not be played forward in the opposition's half of the field.
3. Play with marking defenders.

Hints for instruction

This drill focuses on the decision-making abilities of the player with the ball. This player must adjust his forward dribble each time according to teammates' and opponents' positions.

Variation 1 increases the pressure on the players, which may force them to challenge an opponent. During variation 2 the player with the ball should look to gain space ahead, creating challenge situations. In variation 3, where players will experience constant personal battles, the emphasis should be on the psychological aspect of challenging.

Keywords

Challenging player: assessment, courage, change of tempo

Other members of the team: move away/become available

Topple a Cone

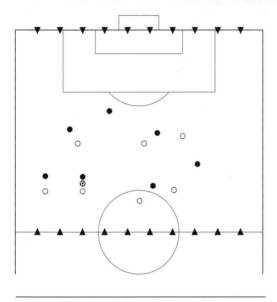

Figure 4.5 Topple a cone.

Pitch

Half the pitch

Players

14—7-v-7

Description

Normal play. Each team defends and attacks a set of 10 cones; one set is placed on the goal line and the other on the halfway line (see figure 4.5).

Scoring

Players score points by hitting one of the opposition's cones.

Variations

1. A point is scored only if the cone tips over.
2. Use two balls in the drill.
3. Introduce a line halfway through the playing area. The ball may enter the attacking zone only if it is dribbled over the halfway line.

Hints for instruction

The drill sets up the players for many challenge situations, because there is a large attacking area. The attacking player must constantly challenge toward a cone and pass the ball on until a good scoring opportunity arises.

Variation 1 forces the player to maintain concentration as she uses more power in the finish. By increasing the number of challenge situations, variation 2 demands better observation from the players. In variation 3 it is important that the players understand that they have to create space for a player who can dribble into the attacking zone.

Keywords

Challenging player: assessment, courage, change of tempo

Other members of the team: move away/become available

No Admittance

Pitch

Half the pitch, with two penalty areas and two full-size goals (see figure 4.6)

Players

16—7 players plus a goalkeeper for each team

Description

Normal play. No one is allowed in the penalty areas, except a player from the attacking team may dribble into the opponent's penalty area to finish (the player is allowed a maximum of two touches in the penalty area).

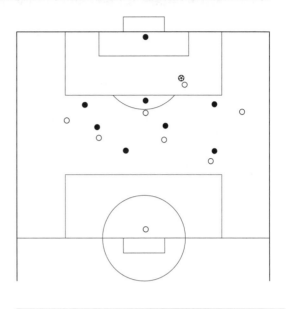

Figure 4.6   No admittance.

Scoring

As normal

Variations

1. A defender may follow the attacker into the penalty area.
2. The defending team may have a player in the penalty area.
3. All players are allowed to enter the penalty area following a breakthrough.

Hints for instruction

The drill encourages the players to try to dribble into the penalty area. The player with the ball must look for and take advantage of opportunities while his teammates get into a position to receive the ball and create space for the player in possession.

Variation 1 makes the finishing situation more realistic and forces the player in possession to shield the ball.

During variation 2 the player with the ball must orient himself as to the position of not only his direct opponent but also of the defender in the area.

Variation 3 focuses on the running patterns and positions of the other members of the team during and after a breakthrough.

Keywords

Challenging player: assessment, courage, change of tempo

Other members of the team: move away/become available

Specific Warm-Up Drills for Practicing Challenging

Slalom Runs

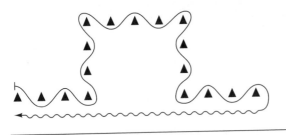

Figure 4.7 Slalom runs.

Players

1

Description

The player dribbles at a good pace around cones, making a short cut every once in a while. On reaching the final cone, the player dribbles at a low pace back to the starting cone (see figure 4.7). The player should dribble using the foot that is farther away from the cone.

Hit the Leg

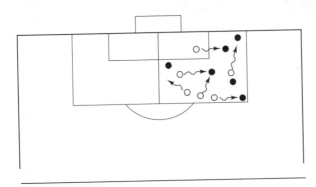

Figure 4.8 Hit the leg.

Pitch

Half the penalty area

Players

12—5 of whom have a ball

Description

Players with a ball dribble and, using the ball, try to hit a player without a ball on the lower leg (see figure 4.8). If a player is hit, that player then takes over the ball and continues dribbling and trying to hit other players.

Green Light

Pitch

A penalty area with three zones

Players

8—6 have a ball and 2 are chasing

Description

Players with a ball must dribble through one of the

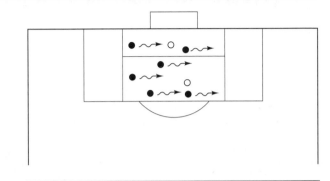

Figure 4.9   Green light.

zones while the chasing players try to win possession. At the coach's signal "forward" or "back," the players should dribble accordingly, forward to the next zone (in the given direction) or back to the area from which they came (always start by signaling "forward"). See figure 4.9.

One-Way Street

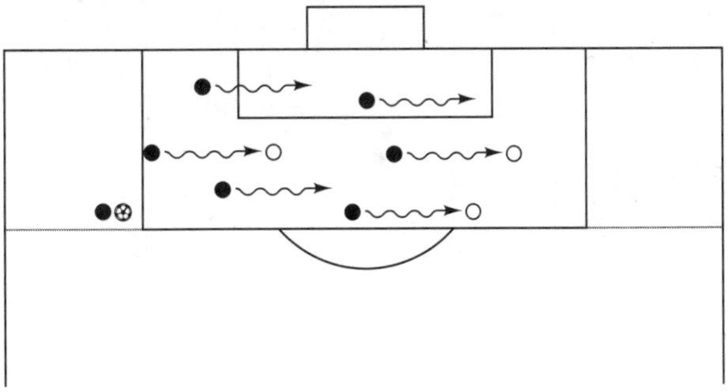

Pitch

About a quarter of the pitch—the penalty area, extended

Players

10—7 have a ball and 3 are chasing

Description

Figure 4.10   One-way street.

The players with a ball should try to dribble through the penalty area to the opposite side, and the three chasing players should try to win the ball (see figure 4.10). Players are permitted to dribble forward and to the side only. A dribbling player may be challenged by only one chasing player at a time. If a chasing player gets the ball, or if the ball is played out of the penalty area, the chasing player takes over the ball. Who can dribble back and forth successfully the most times?

CHAPTER 5

Wall Pass

To bring the ball behind a defender is a key attacking tactic. The wall pass is a commonly used combination between two players when facing a defending player.

Principle

The player with the ball passes to a teammate, who acts as a wall (wall pass player), that is, she passes with one touch to another member of the team. Very often the pass is played back to the player who initially had the ball, on the other side of an opponent (see figure 5.1).

Figure 5.1 Ball back to passing player.

Usage

Wall passes can be carried out all over the pitch, wherever there is open space behind a defender. The wall pass can be very valuable, for example, in breakthrough opportunities for the wingers (see figure 5.2). The wall

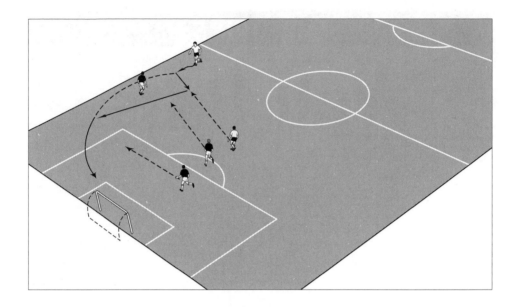

Figure 5.2   Breakthrough opportunity for winger.

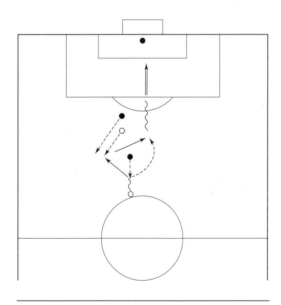

Figure 5.3   Wall pass.

pass provides the opportunity for direct, rapid attacking play with a reduced risk of losing the ball. It is also a tool to use to bring a closely marked teammate in play (see figure 5.3). It is also used to confuse the opposition. A feinted and uncompleted wall pass combination can be an effective attacking action.

A variation of the wall pass is triangle play, where the wall pass player is level with the player with the ball. Figure 5.4 shows an example of triangle play. In 2-v-1 situations, the

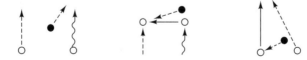

Figure 5.4   Triangle play.

player with the ball dribbles forward at an angle toward the defender. When the player with the ball is a short distance from the defender, he passes to the teammate (wall pass player), who passes the ball forward with his first touch.

Aims

1. To play around a marking defender
2. To create rapid changes of position for the player in possession of the ball
3. To use a closely marked player as a passer

General Description and Hints for Instruction

The wall pass is a simple and effective combination but is technically demanding. Rhythm in execution is important to its effectiveness. The signal for the wall pass can come from either the player with the ball or the wall pass player. The player with the ball can start a wall pass by making contact with the wall pass player, such as with eye contact or with her movement. Equally, a teammate can create the conditions for a combination through her movement (see figure 5.5). For an action to be effective, it is important that the player in possession of the ball rapidly perceive the signal.

Figure 5.5   Combination play.

Main Points for the Player With the Ball

Challenge

The player with the ball should challenge a defender.

Timing of the pass

The player with the ball should pass when the defender facing him is unable to block the pass (a distance of approximately two meters). The ball should not be passed so early as to give the defender the opportunity to intercept the pass from the wall pass player.

The pass

The pass should be firm and along the ground to the wall pass player's far foot. It is better for the player with the ball to use the foot nearer the wall pass player (passing foot). Outside or inside passes are the most effective passing forms.

Change of tempo

Though the player with the ball can run toward the defender with moderate speed, it is important that the pass be followed by acceleration and a sprint past the opponent. In this way the open space behind the defender can be used.

Main Points for the Wall Pass Player

Pattern of movement

The wall pass player must make herself available, for example, by moving first away from the player with the ball and then toward her.

Timing of movement

The wall pass player must adapt her run to the position of the player with the ball and show herself at the right time.

Distance

When receiving the ball, the wall pass player must be quite close (5–10 meters) to the player with the ball, and behind and at an angle to the defender meeting the player with the ball. The wall pass player must face the player with the ball, with her side partly turned to her marker (shielding).

The pass

The wall pass player should pass the first time, ideally with the foot farther from the player with the ball (passing foot); this creates as wide an angle as possible. An inside pass is preferable, but other passes, such as an outside pass, can be used.

Rhythm of Wall Passing

Pitch

Half the pitch and a full-size goal

Players

3—a midfielder (7), a wall pass player (10), and a goalkeeper (1)

Special conditions

A cone, representing a defender, is placed outside the penalty area.

Description

7 dribbles toward the cone and completes a wall pass with 10, after which 7 finishes on goal (see figure 5.6).

Variations

1. A player replaces the cone and acts as a defender (4). 4 should move toward 7.

2. One more defender (5), who passively marks 10, enters the game.

3. 4 and 5 become active; however, they are not allowed to move backward. 7 does not necessarily have to pass to 10.

4. The same conditions apply as in variation 3, but 4 and 5 are permitted to move backward. 10 plays within an area about the size of an extended penalty area, and 5 must follow him. 7 is not allowed to be challenged more than 15 meters from the penalty area.

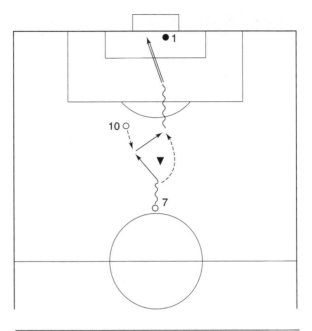

Figure 5.6   Rhythm of wall passing.

Hints for instruction

In the first part of the drill the focus is on the player with the ball changing speed once she has passed to the wall pass player; first she dribbles slowly, then she passes, then she sprints past the opponent (the cone). In addition, the players should get an idea of the movement patterns and passing angles in the wall pass.

In variation 1 the emphasis is on the timing of the pass, the type of pass, and the passing foot. Variation 2 focuses on the wall pass player's type of pass and passing foot, as well as his position relative to the defenders.

Variations 3 and 4 increase the demands on the player with the ball and the wall pass player. The players are forced to be aware of their teammates' and their opponents' positions. Further, attention can be drawn to the wall pass player's movements preceding the wall pass, which lead away from the player with the ball.

Keywords

Player with the ball: challenge, timing of the pass, passing foot, passing form, change of tempo

Wall pass player: timing of movement, pattern of movement, distance, shielding, passing foot, passing form

Focus Game

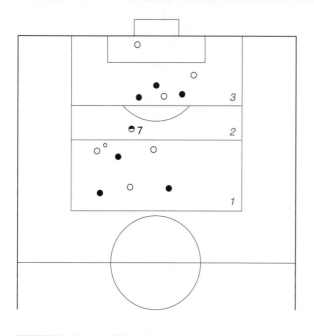

Figure 5.7 Focus game.

Pitch

About a third of the pitch, divided into two wide zones (1 and 3) and one central zone (2)

Players

13—6-v-6, and one wall pass player (7)

Description

7 starts in the central zone, while three players from each team are positioned in each of the wide zones.

The teams must try to play the ball across to the opposite zone via 7. 7 is allowed to pass the ball back to the wide zone from which the ball came (see figure 5.7).

Special rules

Only 7 is allowed to touch the ball in the central zone, and she is allowed only one touch (one-touch play). The players may run from one wide zone to another only after passing to 7. A player who passes to 7 must make a run to the opposite wide zone.

Scoring

The teams score points by playing the ball to the other wide zone, via 7.

Variations

1. The player who passes to 7 can choose whether to head for the opposite zone.

2. Two wall pass players (which means an additional player is introduced into the drill) play for one team each. If the wall pass player wins the ball, he must pass to a teammate (wall pass players may take no more than two touches).

3. Use four wall pass players, two of which play for one team and two for the other (i.e., introduce three extra players into the drill).

Hints for instruction

The drill focuses on the teamwork between the player with the ball, the wall pass player (7), and other team members. The teammates of the player with the ball and the wall pass player should understand the importance of their roles in creating a successful wall pass. Teammates in the opposite zone should either make themselves playable or try to lure the defenders away (create space), so that there will be space for the player who starts the wall pass. Ask your players, "What can you do to make it possible to carry out a successful wall pass?"

Variation 1 should train the player with the ball to assess when it is suitable to carry out the wall pass. If the player in possession of the ball runs to the opposite wide zone after making a pass and the ball is played back to the wide zone from which it came, the team will be down in numbers.

Once the players have got the hang of the practice, variation 2 can be implemented, and then variation 3, in which the demands on the wall pass players increase.

Keywords

Player with the ball: challenge, timing of the pass, passing foot, passing form, change of tempo

Wall-pass player: timing of movement, pattern of movement, distance, shielding, passing foot, passing form

Moving Drill

Pitch

Half the pitch, divided in three zones—a central zone (2) and attacking and defending zones (1 and 3); two full-size goals

Players

14—7-v-7, of whom two players (9 and 10) from each team act as wall pass players. Each team plays with a goalkeeper.

Description

Normal play

Special rules

When the opponent has the ball, 9 and 10 must stay in the attacking zone. Only 9 and 10 are allowed to touch the ball in the central

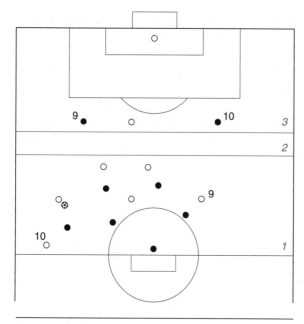

Figure 5.8 Moving drill.

zone, and they are permitted only one touch. The teams can play the ball into the attacking zone only after either 9 or 10 has touched the ball in the central zone (wall pass). See figure 5.8.

Scoring

As normal

Variations

1. 9 and 10 are marked. The markers are allowed to play the ball into the central zone.

2. The number of wall pass players increases to, for example, four on each team, and the wall pass players are allowed to move around the whole pitch.

3. All players may act as wall pass players.

Hints for instruction

In this drill the focus is mainly on the wall pass player's movements toward the player with the ball.

During variation 1, the demands on the wall pass players increase. Introduce this variation once the wall pass players understand the movement pattern.

Variations 2 and 3 increase the number of players who can act as wall pass players and therefore put greater demands on the players to be aware of their surroundings.

Keywords

Player with the ball: challenge, timing of the pass, passing foot, passing form, change of tempo

Wall pass player: timing of movement, pattern of movement, distance, shielding, passing foot, passing form

Joker Alternatives

Pitch

About a third of the pitch, with two small goals at each end

Players

13—5-v-5, plus three floaters who play with the team in possession of the ball

Description

Normal play; each team defends and attacks two small goals (see figure 5.9).

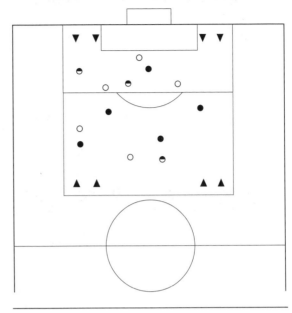

Figure 5.9 Joker alternatives.

Special conditions

The floaters are allowed only one touch.

Scoring

Goals are scored in one of the two small goals.

Variations

1. There are no floaters. Instead, select two players on each team who are allowed to have only one touch on the ball.
2. Both teams play with marking defenders.
3. Goals are scored from a wall pass through one of the goals.

Hints for instruction

The emphasis in this drill is on the possibility of using another team member as a wall pass player. Ask, for example, "When and how can the wall pass be played with the floaters?" Be aware that the quality of the wall pass can be poor if the player with the ball dribbles too close to the wall pass player.

During variation 1 the players must gain an understanding of how another team member can be utilized as a wall pass player. Variation 2 increases the need for wall passes. In variation 3 the change of tempo following a pass to the wall pass player becomes crucial.

Keywords

Player with the ball: challenge, timing of the pass, passing foot, passing form, change of tempo

Wall pass player: timing of movement, pattern of movement, distance, shielding, passing foot, passing form

Specific Warm-Up Drills for Practicing the Wall Pass

Basic Wall Passing

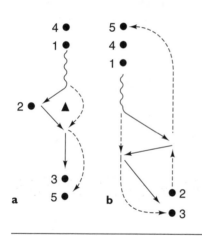

Figure 5.10 Basic wall passing.

Players

5

Description

1 dribbles forward and, just before a cone, passes to 2, who passes one-touch back to 1 on the other side of the cone. 1 then plays the ball to 3, who dribbles forward and passes the ball back to 2, who one-touch passes, and so on. After 1 has passed to 3, she runs behind the line from which 3 started (figure 5.10a).

1 dribbles forward and passes the ball to 2, who runs toward 1. 2 passes one-touch to 1, who plays it one-touch to 3, who dribbles forward and passes to 4, who runs toward 3. 4 plays one-touch to 3, who with one touch passes to 5, and so on. After player 1 has passed to 3, 1 runs back into 3's line while 2 runs to the back of 4's line (5.10b).

Square Drill

Players

    5

Description

The ball is passed with one touch at all times. After passing, the player runs to the corner where the pass went (5.11a).

2 and 4 remain in their own corners. 1 plays 2, who with one touch passes to 3, who has made a run to the corner that 5 has just vacated. 3 passes to 4 who plays a one-touch pass to 5, who, having made a run around 4, runs to the corner that 2 has just left. 5 plays to 2, who plays 1 the first time, and so on (5.11b).

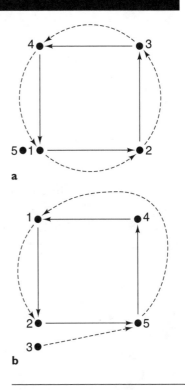

Figure 5.11   Square drill.

Eye Contact

Pitch

    Penalty area

Players

    10, half of whom have a ball

Description

The players with a ball dribble around between the rest of the players inside

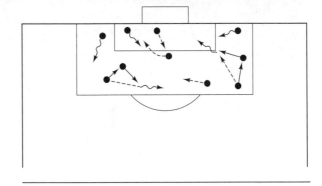

Figure 5.12   Eye contact.

the penalty area. At eye contact, a player with a ball starts a wall pass with a player without a ball. After a set length of time players switch roles (see figure 5.12). In this drill the attention can be on change of tempo. The drill can also be used to reinforce the important concepts involved in using the wall pass.

CHAPTER 6

Overlap

Wide runs to the side of the player dribbling the ball are an effective weapon for creating depth and width in the attacking play.

Principle

A player approaching from behind (overlapping player) overtakes a teammate who has the ball (see figure 6.1).

Figure 6.1 Overlapping player.

Usage

Overlap is used mainly in the opposition's half of the pitch and is an effective weapon for creating depth and width in the attacking play. Opportunities for overlap occur especially along the sidelines, where a fullback or a midfielder can act as the overlapping player (see figure 6.2). The fullback's movements are usually in a direct line, whereas the midfielder tends more often to come from the center and move, at an angle, wide and around the player with the ball. During the 2002 World Cup, the Brazilian team made effective use of overlap. With teamwork on both the right and left sides, Roberto Carlos and Cafu made very dynamic overlap runs. In particular,

Roberto Carlos, the left back, took advantage of his speed to effect overlaps down the line when a midfielder was in possession of the ball. An overlap can also be carried out by a striker who drops off and around the player with the ball (overlap variation; see figure 6.3). This type of overlap is especially effective when the player with the ball is having difficulty finding passing opportunities because some of his teammates are level with him.

When a defender sees or senses the opportunity for an overlap, he often hesitates, which means that the player with the ball is allowed

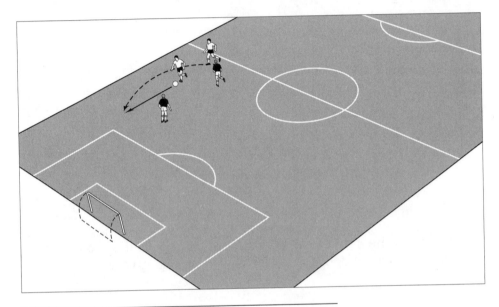

Figure 6.2 Fullback or midfielder acting as the overlapping player.

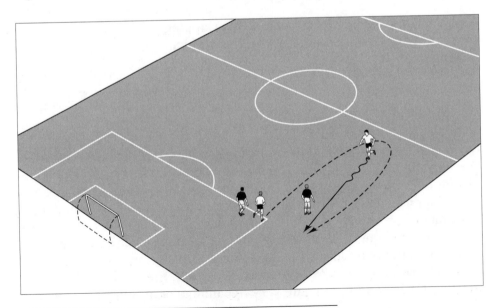

Figure 6.3 Overlap variation.

space to dribble. Figure 6.4 shows how an overlapping player puts a confronting defender, black 2, in a dilemma. If the supporting player runs wide toward the overlapping player, he gives space to the player with the ball; if he does the opposite, the overlapping player will gain space. Many soccer enthusiasts remember the Brazilian Falcao's goal against Italy during the 1982 World Cup—one of the most striking examples of the use of overlap. Falcao had the ball on the edge of the penalty area and faked

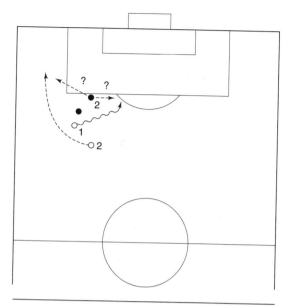

Figure 6.4 Defender dilemma.

a pass to a teammate who made an overlap. By faking, Falcao managed to get three Italian defenders to move outside toward the overlapping player while he made a decisive move in the opposite direction, smacked the ball behind the goalkeeper with his left foot, and put Brazil even at 2-2.

Aims

1. To use an open space and get into a receiving position
2. To give the player with the ball an immediate passing opportunity
3. To divert the defender's attention

General Description and Hints for Instruction

Main Points for the Player With the Ball

Attention

The player with the ball must gain the attention of the defender and lure her slightly away from the area to be used.

Distance

To prevent the defender from being able to mark both the player with the ball and the overlapping player, the player with the ball must be close to the defender. She must also, however, keep enough distance between herself and the defender so that the defender is unable to block the ball as it is being passed to the overlapping player.

Assessment

The moment the defender is level with the player in possession of the ball, the player with the ball must decide whether to pass to the overlapping player or move in the opposite direction and thereby take advantage of the confusion his teammate has created.

The pass

If the player with the ball chooses to pass, she must play the ball into the open area at a certain time so that the overlapping player can use her speed and continue her run directly into the path of the ball (timing of the pass). If the pass is made too early, the defender may be able to interfere. If the pass comes in too late, there is a risk that either the overlapping player will run into an offside position, or the defender can cover it because the angle of the pass is too small. The ball should be played with the foot that is closer to the open area to avoid giving the defender a chance to interfere (passing foot). Passing with the outside of the foot is often the preferable passing form.

Main Points for the Overlapping Player

Distance to player with the ball

The overlapping player must run past the player with the ball at a suitable distance (2 to 10 meters) so that the defender's ability to cover the player with the ball and to block the pass is decreased.

Change of tempo

The overlapping player runs at a high speed to use the free space.

Signal

The overlapping player can tell the player in possession—for example, with a call—when to play the ball. That moment will often be when the overlapping player is level with the player with the ball.

Timing of the Run

Pitch

About a third of the pitch and a full-size goal

Players

4—a striker (11); a midfielder (over-lapping player, 7); a defender (5), who marks 11; and a goalkeeper (1)

Description

11 runs indirectly toward 7, who passes to 11. 11 turns and dribbles slowly toward the center. 11 passes to 7 in the instant that 7 comes

around behind her. From there 7 dribbles to the goal line and crosses to 11 (see figure 6.5).

Scoring

As normal

Variations

1. 5 does not have to follow 11. 11 is not forced to play 7.

2. One extra defender (6), who marks 7, is introduced into the game.

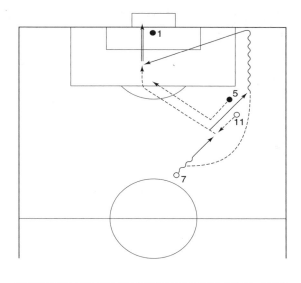

Figure 6.5 Timing of the run.

3. 7 starts off farther up the field than 11 and, after a pass to 11, 7 makes a run behind 11 and wide toward the sideline (overlap variation; see figure 6.5).

Hints for instruction

In the first part of the drill the focus is primarily on the timing of the pass (including the signal from 7), the player with the ball's passing foot and form, and the overlapping player's pattern of movement relative to the player with the ball. It may be beneficial for 7 to run in an arc around the player with the ball to give him more time and space to make the pass, as well as to avoid running into an offside position.

During variation 1 the players must gain an understanding of how the overlap can be used to confuse the defender, and the player with the ball must get an idea of when it would be wise to keep the ball and dribble.

Variation 2 focuses on the necessity for 7 to run at a high speed so as to use the open space. During variation 3 the players should gain an understanding of how they can put 6 out of the play by executing the overlap in the correct manner.

Keywords

Player with the ball: attention, distance to opponent, assessment, timing of the pass, passing foot, passing form

Overlapping player: distance to player with the ball, change of tempo, signal

Triple Overlap

Figure 6.6 Triple overlap.

Pitch

About half the pitch and a full-size goal

Players

8—two strikers (10 and 11); two midfielders (7 and 9); three defenders (2, 5, and 6), of whom 2 and 5 are marking 10 and 11; and a goalkeeper

Description

10 makes a run toward 7, who passes to 10 and runs forward. At the same time that the pass comes from 7, 9 overlaps around 10, who moves inside with the ball and passes wide to 9. 9 dribbles to the goal line and crosses the ball in to 7, 10, or 11, who have all made runs into the penalty area (10 and 11 effect a crossover; see page 79). See figure 6.6.

Scoring

As normal

Variations

1. 7 and 9 pass to each other while 6 tries to intercept the ball. At a given time either 7 or 9 passes the ball to 10 or 11, respectively. When 7 passes to 10, 9 is executing an overlap outside of 10; similarly, number 7 completes an overlap on the outside of 11 if 9 passes to 11.

2. 10 and 11 are not forced to play the ball on; they have the option to dribble with the ball.

3. 2 and 5 are not restricted to following 10 and 11.

Hints for instruction

This drill is a variation from Timing of the Run (page 57), which gradually approaches a true game situation. The drill should develop the players' understanding of how to use overlap in game situations.

During variations 2 and 3 the coach can emphasize the possibilities that faking an overlap can present.

Keywords

Player with the ball: attention, distance to opponent, assessment, timing of the pass, passing foot, passing form

Overlapping player: distance to player with the ball, change of tempo, signal

Counting Overlaps

Pitch

Half the penalty area, divided into four zones

Players

4—three attackers (1, 2, 3) and one player chasing the ball (4)

Special conditions

One attacker starts in each zone while the defender is allowed to move freely over the whole playing area.

Description

The attackers who are not in possession of the ball must stay in the zones adjacent to the one where the ball is. The attackers pass to each other while the chasing player tries to intercept the ball. The player with the ball makes a pass and then runs around the player she passed to and into the next zone (overlap). The player now in possession of the ball should pass to the overlapping player as soon as the overlapping player has overtaken her. See figure 6.7.

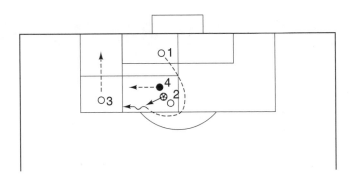

Figure 6.7 Counting overlaps.

Scoring

Count the number of successful overlaps, that is, instances when the ball has been played (not necessarily to the overlapping player) after the overlap without the chasing player gaining possession.

Variations

1. The attackers have a limited number of touches, such as a maximum of five.
2. The attackers must carry out an overlap after at least every three passes.

Hints for instruction

Of all the general principles concerning overlap, the focus in this drill is the overlapping player's change of speed. To give the player with the ball two passing options, the overlapping player quickly needs to gets himself into a passing position. To keep players working at a high level of intensity, give the players a rest when they switch with the defender. Formal breaks can possibly be implemented (interval principle).

The objective of this drill is also to give the player with the ball an understanding of when it is wise to pass to the overlapping player and when it is better to keep the ball at one's feet. The player's choice depends on, among other things, the position of the defender.

Variation 1 increases still further the need for a quick overlap. Variation 2 ensures execution of the overlap; however, the drill is quite physically demanding, and it may be necessary to introduce longer breaks.

Keywords

Player with the ball: attention, distance to opponent, assessment, timing of the pass, passing foot, passing form

Overlapping player: distance to player with the ball, change of tempo, signal

Rugby Drill

Pitch

Half the pitch

Players

14—7-v-7

Description

As normal

Special condition

A forward pass can be received only by a teammate who is in line with or behind the ball when it is passed (see figure 6.8).

Scoring

The teams score points by dribbling over the opposition's goal line (goal line/center line).

Variation

A forward pass can be received only by a teammate who was in front of the ball when the player in possession received the ball, and who has been behind the player with the ball before receiving.

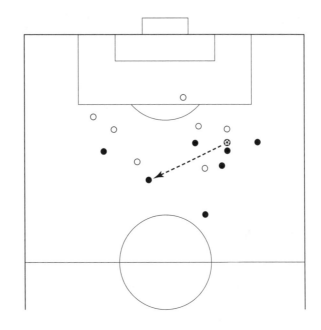

Figure 6.8 Rugby drill variation.

Hints for instruction

The drill should help the players to assess how and when they can put themselves into a free position by overlapping. It is important that the players have a lot of space to carry out a tactically correct overlap; therefore, make sure that both the playing and goal areas are large relative to the number of players.

The variation focuses on the overlap variation (see figure 6.3 on page 54).

Keywords

Player with the ball: attention, distance to opponent, assessment, timing of the pass, passing foot, passing form

Overlapping player: distance to player with the ball, change of tempo, signal

Channel Opportunity

Pitch

About three-quarters of the pitch, with a halfway line and two wide zones (channels) along the sides (see figure 6.9); two full-size goals

Players

18—8-v-8, plus a goalkeeper on each team

Description

Normal play

Special conditions

No players are allowed in the channels on their own half of the field. The attacking team cannot play the ball out to one of the channels before the ball has crossed the halfway line. One player from the attacking team is positioned in the channels. A player can enter a channel only after the ball has been played into it, and only if he was farther down the field than the player who passed the ball.

Scoring

As normal

Variations

1. A goal is accepted only if the ball has been played in one of the channels at some time during the attacking phase.
2. A goal counts double if it follows a pass coming from one of the channels.
3. The ball is not allowed to come to a standstill in the channels, and the ball can be touched only a maximum of five times in the channels.
4. There is no halfway line and the ball can be played out to the channels at any time.
5. Each team selects overlapping players who are the only ones allowed in the channels, and even they may not enter until the conditions are fulfilled.
6. The defending team is also allowed one player in the channels, but only if the attacking team has a player there already (the channels are made wider).

Hints for instruction

In this drill the players must gain an understanding of the opportunities the overlap gives them. Increasing the width of the channels and

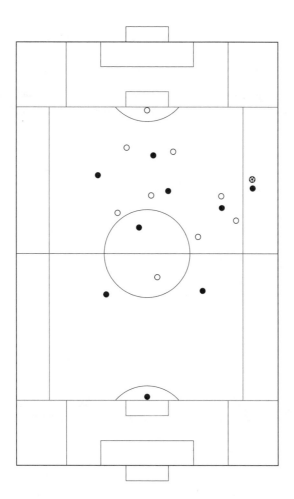

Figure 6.9 Channel opportunity.

implementing variations 1 and 2 provide opportunities for the number of overlaps to increase. It can be necessary to make use of variation 3 to avoid the play in the channels becoming ungamelike. Variation 4 should give the players an idea of how to use overlaps all over the field.

Variation 5 limits the number of possible overlapping players, which makes it easier for the overlapping players to anticipate. Variation 6 places a greater demand on the players to remain aware of their surroundings, in that they must assess when it is appropriate to pass to the overlapping player.

Keywords

Player with the ball: attention, distance to opponent, assessment, timing of the pass, passing foot, passing form

Overlapping player: distance to player with the ball, change of tempo, signal

Specific Warm-Up Drills for Practicing Overlaps

Overlap on Line

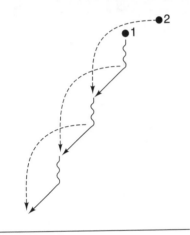

Players

2

Description

1 dribbles forward and, when she can glimpse 2, makes a diagonal forward pass to 2. 2 dribbles forward and passes diagonally forward to 1, and so on. See figure 6.10.

Figure 6.10 Overlap on line.

Three in a Row

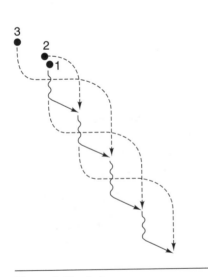

Figure 6.11 A threesome.

Players

3

Description

1 dribbles forward and passes a diagonal ball forward to 2 when 2 becomes visible. 2 dribbles forward and makes an angled pass forward to 3, who runs around behind both 1 and 2. 3 dribbles forward and passes forward to 1, who has made a run around 2 and 3. 1 dribbles forward, passes diagonally forward to 2, who has made a run around 1 and 3; 2 dribbles forward, and so on. See figure 6.11.

Waiting for an Overlap

Pitch

Extended penalty area

Players

10, half of whom have a ball

Description

The players with a ball dribble among the rest of the players in the area. The players without a ball (overlapping players) must move around a player with the ball and, by calling, indicate that the player in possession should pass. The overlapping player dribbles on until another player makes an overlap. See figure 6.12.

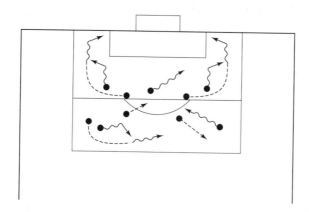

Figure 6.12 Waiting for an overlap.

CHAPTER 7

Takeover

Changing the direction of the game can often make it hard for the opponents to defend. In switching the ball between two teammates, the player taking over the ball changes the game and has a good opportunity to win ground over his direct opponent.

Principle

A player who is dribbling allows an incoming teammate (takeover player) to take over the ball (see figure 7.1).

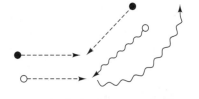

Figure 7.1 Takeover player gets ball.

Usage

The takeover can be carried out anywhere on the field to give the player who has taken over the ball a better position to penetrate. By making a move just after the takeover, the player who now has the ball has a good opportunity to win ground over his direct opponent. Takeovers can also be used to confuse the opposition. A feinted or uncompleted takeover can be an effective method of attack.

The takeover can be carried out both parallel to the opposition's goal line (parallel takeover; see figure 7.1) and in depth, or lengthwise up the field (depth takeover; see figure 7.2). A variation of the takeover is the diagonal cross takeover, where the takeover player runs behind the player with the ball and on the far side of that player's direct opponent (see figure 7.3). In this case—in contrast to the traditional takeover—the player with the ball must gently nudge the ball into position for the takeover player.

Figure 7.2 Depth takeover.   **Figure 7.3** Diagonal cross takeover.

Aims

1. To use a free space
2. To shield an opponent
3. To confuse opponents
4. To vary the game
5. To help a player under pressure

General Description and Hints for Instruction

By luring her direct opponent with her as she dribbles, the player with the ball creates free space that another member of the team (takeover player) can exploit.

Main Points for the Player With the Ball

Communication

For a takeover to succeed, close communication, such as eye contact, should occur between the two players. By dribbling toward a teammate, the player with the ball can signal that he wants that player to take over the ball.

Dribbling speed

The player with the ball should be running slowly enough for the marking player to be able to keep up, so that a space is created behind the player with the ball.

Dribbling foot

To protect the ball, the player in possession should dribble with the foot that is farther from the defender.

Leave the ball

The player with the ball should run over the ball or let it roll. A common error in takeovers occurs when the player with the ball prods the ball a little just before the takeover, which makes it more difficult for the takeover player to get hold of the ball.

Change of tempo

After letting go of the ball, the player should continue in a break so as to lure his direct opponent away from the player who has taken over the ball.

Main Points for the Takeover Player

Timing

The takeover player must adapt her run in coordination with the player with the ball, so that she "asks" for the ball at the right time.

Position

The takeover player must take over the ball as far away as possible from his opponent. A common error occurs when the ball is taken over between the takeover player and his marker, and the takeover player runs into the defender.

Takeover foot

The takeover player must take over the ball with the foot that is closer to the player with the ball, that is, the same foot that the player with the ball is using to dribble.

Change of tempo

The takeover player must break with the ball.

Basic Takeover

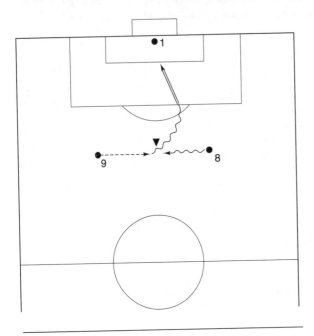

Pitch

About a third of the pitch and one full-size goal

Players

3—two strikers (8 and 9) and a goalkeeper (1)

Description

8 dribbles across to the cone, where 9 takes over the ball and takes a couple of steps before fin-ishing (see figure 7.4).

Figure 7.4 Basic takeover.

Variations

1. The cone is removed. Add a defender (3), who marks 8.
2. 8 and 9 may choose which of them continues with the ball. 3 can decide for herself if she wants to follow 8 or 9.
3. Add another defender, who marks 9.

Hints for instruction

In the first part of the drill the focus is on 8's and 9's positions relative to each other, on the dribbling foot and the takeover foot, as well as on the point at which 8 must leave the ball.

Variation 1 increases the demands on the players, and the points just mentioned become even more relevant. The variation also emphasizes the timing between the two players.

During variation 2 the players must evaluate whether it is advantageous to complete or fake a takeover.

Variation 3 can give the players an understanding of the options available when executing a takeover. In particular, draw attention to the necessary change of speed that allows the takeover player to use the free space created.

Keywords

The player with the ball: communication, dribbling speed, dribbling foot, leave the ball, change of tempo

The takeover player: timing, position, takeover foot, change of tempo

Neighbor Help

Pitch

Half the penalty area, divided into four zones of equal size

Players

5—four strikers (1–4) and one player chasing the ball (5)

Special conditions

The attackers start off each in a separate zone, and one of them has a ball. 5 starts in the same zone as the ball.

Description

One of the players from an adjacent zone must complete a takeover with the player in possession of the ball. After the takeover the ball is dribbled to an adjacent zone, and the player chasing the ball follows. When 5 wins the ball, the attacker who lost it becomes the new chasing player. See figure 7.5.

Special rule

No more than two attackers can be in any one zone at the same time.

Scoring

Count the number of takeovers completed before the chasing player wins the ball.

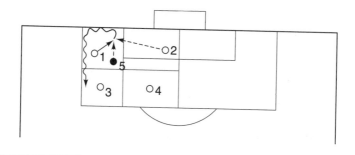

Figure 7.5   Neighbor help.

Variations

1. The defender needs only to touch the ball to become an attacker.
2. Several takeovers may take place in the same zone, for example, 1 can take over the ball from 2 again (see figure 7.5). The player with the ball thus has two zones into which he can dribble.

Hints for instruction

In this drill the attention is mainly on the players' individual positions during the takeover, as well as the dribbling foot and takeover foot.

Keywords

The player with the ball: communication, dribbling speed, dribbling foot, leave the ball, change of tempo

The takeover player: timing, position, takeover foot, change of tempo

Steal the Ball

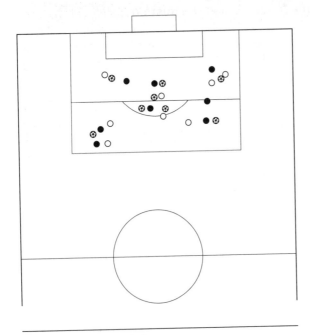

Figure 7.6 Steal the ball.

Pitch

An extended penalty area

Players

16—8-v-8

Special conditions

Four players on each team have a ball (see figure 7.6).

Description

The players on each team must try to gain a ball from the opposition while keeping their own balls within the team's possession.

Special rule

Passing the ball is prohibited; a teammate can receive the ball only through a takeover.

Scoring

The team in possession of more balls after a given time, such as every minute, gets four points.

Variation

Each team starts with two balls, and a team scores one point when they have three in their possession.

Hints for instruction

In this drill the players should accustom themselves to helping a teammate by completing a takeover and to looking to a teammate for help in taking over the ball.

The variation increases the pressure on the player in possession of the ball, and consequently the need for takeovers increases as well.

Keywords

The player with the ball: communication, dribbling speed, dribbling foot, leave the ball, change of tempo

The takeover player: timing, position, takeover foot, change of tempo

Crossing the Line

Pitch

Half the pitch

Players

14—7-v-7

Description

Normal play

Special rule

The ball can be moved forward only through dribbling, that is, it cannot be played forward.

Scoring

The teams score points by dribbling over the opposition's goal line (goal line/halfway line). See figure 7.7.

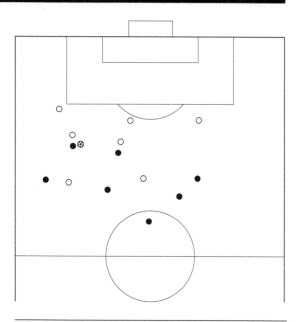

Figure 7.7 Crossing the line.

Variations

1. The ball may not be played backward.
2. The special rule applies only in a central zone (about 20 meters wide).

Hints for instruction

In this drill the players must gain an understanding of how they can aid a teammate by offering themselves as takeover players. Because the teams play in a certain attacking direction, the drill also presents the opportunity to focus on the players' positions relative to their opponents'.

Keywords

The player with the ball: communication, dribbling speed, dribbling foot, leave the ball, change of tempo

The takeover player: timing, position, takeover foot, change of tempo

Bring the Ball Home

Pitch

Extended penalty area, divided into two zones (1 and 2)

Players

8—4-v-4

Description

Each team has a home zone in which they must seek to maintain possession of the ball. When a team wins the ball from the opposition, it can be played into the home zone only once a takeover has been completed. See figure 7.8.

Scoring

The teams score points by effecting 10 passes in their home zone without the opposition gaining the ball.

Variation

Each team has one extra player who starts outside the drill area. When a team gets possession of the ball in the opposition's home zone, their extra player steps into the game so they are now playing 5-v-4. When the ball has been played across to the other home zone, the player who won the ball acts as the new extra player and starts the next round outside the drill area.

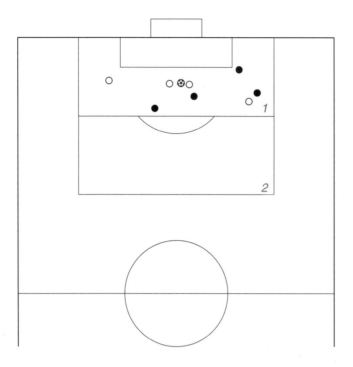

Figure 7.8   Bring the ball home.

Hints for instruction

Once the ball has been won, it is important that the player with the ball invite a takeover and that some of her teammates move toward her. The takeover is followed by a forward-looking direction of play (toward the home zone). The drill thus brings in an important part of the transition from defense to attack: moving away from area where the ball has been regained. The change of tempo becomes important for the team to make use of the open space in the other zone.

The variation can give the takeover extra speed, in that the new player can adjust his run to the game situation.

Keywords

The player with the ball: communication, dribbling speed, dribbling foot, leave the ball, change of tempo

The takeover player: timing, position, takeover foot, change of tempo

Specific Warm-Up Drills for Practicing Takeovers

Relay Drill

Players

4

Description

1 dribbles toward 2, who, after running toward 1, takes over the ball and dribbles to meet 3, who, after running toward 2, takes over the ball, and so on. See figure 7.9.

Figure 7.9 Relay drill.

Continuous Takeover

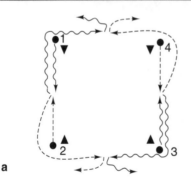

a

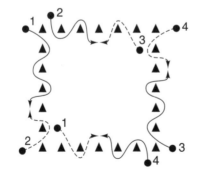

b

Figure 7.10 Continuous takeover.

Pitch

Square (15 by 15 meters)

Players

4

Description

1 and 3, each with a ball and starting at the same time, dribble toward 2 and 4, who run toward 1 and 3, respectively (figure 7.10a). When the players meet, 2 and 4 then take over the balls. 2 and 4 continue dribbling until they meet 3 and 1, who take over the balls and dribble until they face 4 and 2, respectively, and so on.

Follow the same procedure as in step 1, but the players have to dribble around cones (figure 7.10b). The cones should represent opponents. Switch regularly between takeovers close to the cones and at a distance from them. The correct takeover position depends on where on the pitch the players meet.

Swap Ball

Pitch

> Penalty area

Players

> 10, half of whom have a ball

Description

> The players in possession of a ball dribble around in the penalty area while the remaining players run among them.
>
> At eye contact two players meet and execute a takeover, and the takeover player continues dribbling until she makes eye contact with another player (see figure 7.11). Draw attention to the takeover foot and the change of tempo. After a while, the coach can designate an attacking direction, so that the players' individual positions at the time of takeover can be analyzed.

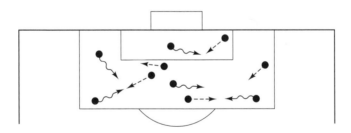

Figure 7.11 Swap ball.

CHAPTER 8

Crossover and Split Runs

In creating or exploiting free space an attacking player always has the initiative. He decides when to do the runs. Combined with a mutual understanding between two or more players, a well-orchestrated move gives scoring opportunities.

Principle

Two teammates' runs cross at high speed (see figure 8.1).

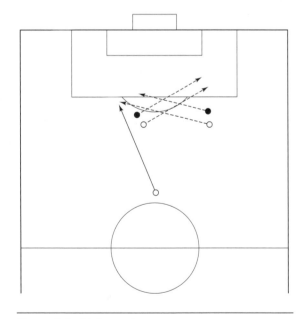

Figure 8.1 High-speed cross.

Usage

Crossovers are used by midfielders, strikers, or both in an attempt to create space for each other or for other team members. They normally take place in the opposition's half of the field, typically when the ball is crossed into the penalty area; one striker runs for the near post and another heads for the far post (see figure 8.2).

The opposite movement pattern appears in the *split run*, where two strikers move away from each other (see figure 8.3). This creates space in the center that, for instance, a midfielder can use. The split run gives the player with the ball the opportunity to pass either to the strikers or into the open area.

Aims

1. To create space for other team members
2. To use the space a teammate has created
3. To create confusion in the opposition's defense
4. To give the player with the ball more passing options

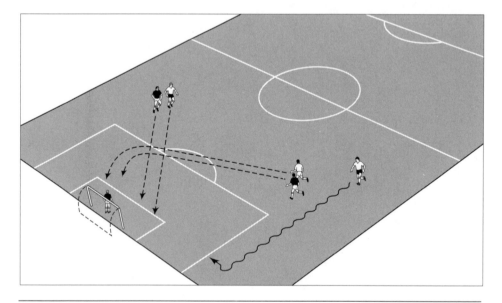

Figure 8.2 Crossover.

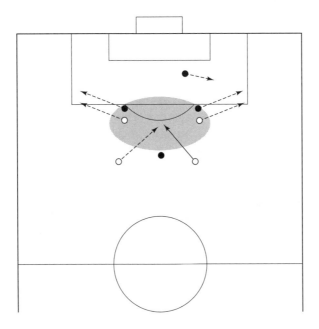

Figure 8.3　Split run.

General Description and Hints for Instruction

Main Points for the Crossover Players

Communication

Communication between the crossover players, as well as between the player with the ball and the crossover players, is essential. For example, the signal for a crossover between two forwards could be a cross pass to a midfielder who makes eye contact with one of the forwards, whose acceleration sets off the other striker. It is preferable that the player positioned on the same side of the field as the ball starts the crossover to open up to the side of the least likely pass.

Change of tempo

The crossover must come as a surprise, and it is therefore important that the forwards accelerate. The break should be a long, diagonal one.

Timing

It is important that when making a crossover in the penalty area before a cross, the players time their movements. The player running to the near post must hesitate so that he arrives at the post at the same time as the ball. The player who heads for the far post must make an indirect run and then, as the ball is coming in, run at high speed toward the post.

Main Point for the Player With the Ball

Timing of the pass

If the pass is aimed at one of the strikers, then the ball must be played early enough so that the crossover player can make his run onto the ball and avoid being caught in an offside position. It is often most appropriate to pass to the crossover player who makes the later run, because he has the opportunity to use the space created by the other crossover player, and because he is often closer to the player with the ball.

Timing of Crossover

Pitch

About half the pitch and a full-size goal

Players

6—two strikers (10 and 11); a midfielder (7); two defenders (3 and 5), who mark 10 and 11; and a goalkeeper (1)

Description

10 runs toward 7, who plays to 10. 10 passes back to 7 and then moves diagonally (behind 11). 7 passes the ball diagonally to 11, who dribbles toward the goal line and crosses the ball to 10 or 7. See figure 8.4.

Scoring

As normal

Variations

1. 10 and 11 may choose which of them moves toward 7 at the beginning of the drill to receive the ball.
2. Bring an extra defender into the drill to act as sweeper.
3. On receiving the ball from 10 or 11, 7 may then choose whether to pass to 10 or 11.

Hints for instruction

In the first part of the drill the focus is mainly on the paths 10 and 11 take, and their changes of tempo.

During variation 1 the emphasis is on communication, including timing, between 7, 10, and 11. 10's or 11's run toward 7 is the signal to start the crossover.

Variation 2 focuses on 7's assessment of the timing and direction of the pass. 10 and 11 should think only about making the crossover

Figure 8.4   Timing of crossover.

as quickly as possible, because 7 is responsible for making the pass to 10 or 11 a good one.

In variation 3, 7 has to judge whether to pass to the crossover players or to dribble.

Keywords

Crossover players: communication, change of tempo, timing

Player with the ball: timing of the pass

Crossover in the Penalty Area

Pitch

About a quarter of the pitch and a full-size goal

Players

4—two strikers (10 and 11), a midfielder (7), and a goalkeeper (1)

Description

7 dribbles toward the goal line while 11 heads toward the near post and 10 runs (behind 11) away from 7 and backward into the box. 7 plays the ball across to either 10 or 11. See figure 8.5.

Scoring

As normal

Variations

1. Add two defenders, who mark 10 and 11.
2. 7 passes after only two touches toward the goal line.

Hints for instruction

In the first part of the drill the emphasis is on 10's and 11's runs and timing in relation to 7's dribbling and cross. 10's and 11's runs should

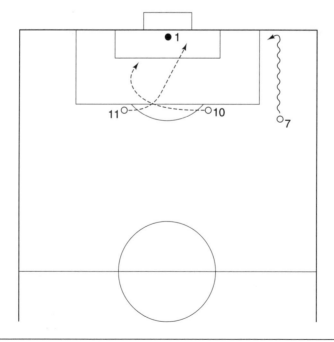

Figure 8.5 Crossover in the penalty area.

be coordinated in relation to actual positions outside the penalty area. To prevent arriving at the near post too early, 11 can run slightly in the opposite direction to 7 and then break toward the post. It is vital for 10 to run in a curve around 11 to get up to high speed in the run toward the ball when the cross comes in.

From variation 1, 10 should gain an understanding of the necessity of changing tempo to escape from the opponent. In variation 2, 10 and 11 must move directly into the box but avoid getting into an offside position.

Keywords

Crossover players: communication, change of tempo, timing

Player with the ball: timing of the pass

Down and Up

Pitch

About a third of the pitch, divided into six zones—two defensive zones, two attacking zones, and two center zones; two full-size goals

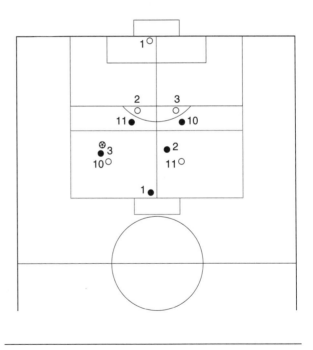

Players

10—5-v-5. Each team consists of two crossover players (10 and 11); two defenders (2 and 3), who mark the opposition's crossover players; and a goalkeeper (1).

Figure 8.6 Down and up.

Special conditions

10 and 11 on each team start off in separate areas of the attacking zones, together with the player marking them. See figure 8.6.

Description

Before the ball can go beyond the center, it must be passed from the defensive zone to either 10 or 11 in the central zone. The player who receives the ball should then play it back to the defender, who then plays it forward to the other crossover player. After this, attack as normal.

Special rules

10 and 11 may not enter their own defensive zones, and when play is in their team's defensive zones, they should remain in their own areas of the attacking zones. The equivalent rules apply to 2 and 3, who mark 11 and 10. 10 and 11 may not win the ball in the central zone, and 2 and 3 may not challenge the first pass to the crossover player.

Scoring

As normal

Variations

1. The crossover player who receives the ball does not have to play the ball back.
2. The defender does not have to play the ball forward after receiving it from a crossover player.
3. Play as in variations 1 and 2, but without marking defenders.

Hints for instruction

In this drill 10 and 11 should understand the advantages of the marker being pushed away from the area.

Variation 1 can elaborate on this concept; the forward-running player can now get himself free. Make sure 10 and 11 are aware that the speed of their runs plays an important part in either their or their teammates' becoming free.

In variations 1, 2, and 3, the players should become accustomed to assessing the situation and making a quick decision. The players should get an idea of the options that the correctly performed crossover provides for the player with the ball.

Keywords

Crossover players: communication, change of tempo, timing

Player with the ball: timing of the pass

Switching Channel

Pitch

About three-quarters of the pitch (from penalty area to penalty area), with a halfway line and two wide zones (channels); two full-size goals

Players

20—8-v-8, plus a goalkeeper for each team. Two players from each team are crossover players (10 and 11).

Description

Normal play

Special rules

10 and 11 should remain in the channels (except during crossing runs) in the attacking zone, and they may touch the ball only in the channels (see figure 8.7). The remaining players may not enter the channels, nor may the ball be left lying in the channels. The first time 10 or 11 receives the ball once it has been won, the player may have only one touch. 10 and 11 should subsequently change channel sides. Play after this is free, until the opposition has regained the ball.

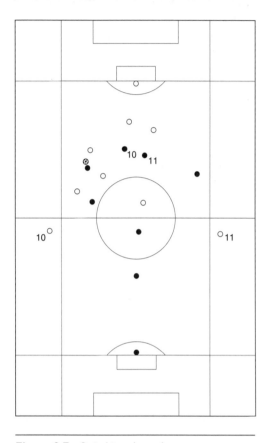

Figure 8.7 Switching channel.

Scoring

As normal

Variations

1. For a goal to be counted, one of the crossover players must have touched the ball in an attack before the goal was scored.
2. A goal following a cross from the channels counts double.
3. 10 and 11 should undertake a crossover immediately after the ball has been regained; after this play is free.

4. 10 and 11 may move freely over the opposition's half of the pitch. Once 10 or 11 has touched the ball twice in one of the channels, they should both run to the opposite channel.

5. Play with no channels but with two players who still may not go onto their own half of the pitch.

Hints for instruction

Apart from introducing the general principles of the crossover, the aim of this drill is for 10 and 11 to become accustomed to running across each other to make themselves available. Moreover, 10 and 11 should understand that by sprinting to the opposite channel, they can become more quickly available.

Introduce variations 1 and 2 if 10 and 11 are not being brought into the game as much as they should be.

Variations 3, 4, and 5 are extensions of the original drill in which the crossover players should get an idea of how they can use the crossover in game situations.

Keywords

Crossover players: communication, change of tempo, timing

Player with the ball: timing of the pass

Specific Warm-Up Drills for Practicing the Crossover

Play and Cross

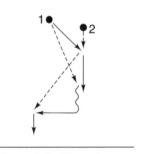

Figure 8.8 Play and cross.

Players

2

Description

1 passes to 2, who plays the ball forward. After passing, 1 runs diagonally forward and 2 runs behind 1. 1 gains the ball and dribbles, then plays the ball across, and so on. After a certain length of time, 1 and 2 switch roles. See figure 8.8.

Continuous Crossovers

Players

3

Description

1 passes to 3, who plays the ball back to 1, who passes in the same direction. Meanwhile, 3 and 2 have performed a crossover, so that 2 receives the ball from 1 (figure 8.9a). Following this, 1 and 3 perform a crossover, and 2 passes forward (figure 8.9b). Play continues in this manner. It may be appropriate to use cones to indicate where the players should run, but avoid this if possible, in that it constrains the players' movements.

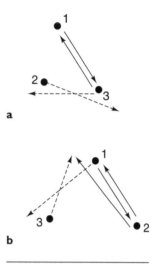

Figure 8.9 Continuous crossovers.

Anthill

Players

4

Description

1 passes to 2, who plays 3, who passes back to 2, who then passes back in the same direction. In the meantime, 3 and 4 have performed a crossover, so that 4 receives the ball from 2 (figure 8.10a). After this, 1 and 2 perform a crossover run, while 4 plays 3, who passes to 1, who plays back to 3 (figure 8.10b), and so on.

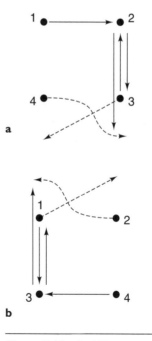

Figure 8.10 Anthill.

CHAPTER 9

Decoy Run

To free oneself from a tight marker requires timing and speed. A decoy run can also be part of creating depth in attacking play and unity between defense, midfield, and attack.

Principle

A *decoy player* runs in the opposite direction from and then toward a teammate who has possession of the ball (see figure 9.1).

Usage

A tightly marked midfielder or attacker can use the decoy run to create free space behind her (see figure 9.2) or to make herself playable. The decoy run can be part of creating depth in attacking play and unity between defense, midfield,

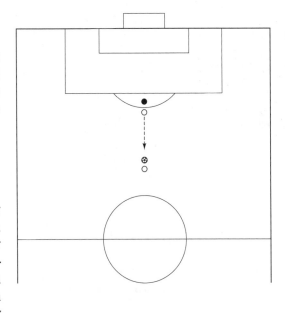

Figure 9.1　Decoy play.

and attack (see page 141). The decoy run is particularly useful when a fullback or midfielder dribbles up toward the penalty area toward a line of teammates.

Aims

1. To create space for other team members
2. To make oneself available
3. To create space for a change in the direction of attack
4. To act as a wall for further combinations

Figure 9.2   A midfielder or attacker uses the decoy run to create free space.

General Description and Hints for Instruction

Main Points for the Decoy Player

Running speed

The running speed of the decoy player is a vital factor in whether the player gets free or a free area is created. With moderate speed, the marker will keep up and space will be created that either the decoy player himself or a teammate can use. If he sprints, he has a chance of receiving the ball in a free position and will have time to control and turn with the ball.

Receiving the ball

On receiving the ball the decoy player has several options.

- He can try to "hide" from his marker by receiving the ball with the foot farther away from his opponent.
- He can fake a movement to one side and dribble to the other.
- He can act as a wall for the player who just passed the ball.
- He can fake taking the ball, let it run between his legs, turn around his teammate, and come up with the ball.

Main Points for the Player With the Ball

Assessment

The player with the ball should assess her passing options. She could play the ball into the free space that the decoy player has created. She could pass to the decoy player according to what she wants to accomplish tactically.

- The decoy player could stay on the ball to bring more team members farther forward on the pitch.
- The decoy player could play the ball back to the player who just passed the ball.
- The decoy player could act as a wall.
- The decoy player could try to turn the direction of the attack.

Open Up

Pitch

About half the pitch and a full-size goal

Players

5—a midfielder (7); two strikers (10 and 11); a defender (3), who marks 11; and a goalkeeper (1)

Description

7 dribbles and passes to 11, who makes a decoy run. 11 immediately plays the ball back to 7, who quickly passes to 10, who has made a run into the space created by 11. 10 dribbles diagonally out toward the goal line and crosses the ball to 7 or 11. See figure 9.3.

Scoring

As normal

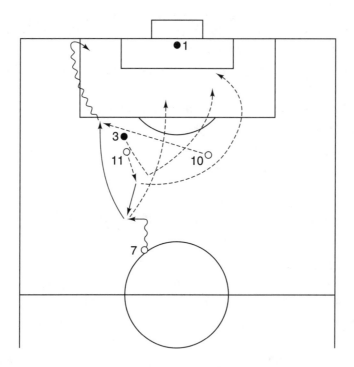

Figure 9.3   Open up.

Variations

1. Add one extra defender, who marks 10.
2. 3 is not forced to follow 11. 7 can choose whether to pass to 10 or 11. After the pass the drill continues under the normal conditions, except that 7 has a maximum of two touches when in contact with the ball.
3. Introduce another defender, who marks 7. After the pass to 10 or 11, the drill continues under the normal conditions for all players.

Hints for instruction

In the first part of the drill the focus is mainly on the speed of 11's run and on 10's opportunities for using the space created by 11.

During variation 1 it is important that 10 does not start too early; doing so will limit his space at the moment when he receives the delivery from 7. In variations 2 and 3 the emphasis is on the considerations 7 must make concerning 10's and 11's roles in receiving the ball. In particular, the option of using 10 or 11 as a wall ought to become clear.

Keywords

Decoy player: running speed, receiving the ball

Player with the ball: assessment

Cone Scoring

Pitch

About one-fifth of the pitch, divided into four zones—two wide zones (1 and 4) and two central zones (2 and 3)

Players

8—4-v-4, with two attackers (10 and 11) and two defenders (3 and 4) on each team

Special conditions

Two players only from each team must be on their own half of the pitch (zones 1 + 2 and 3 + 4).

Description

When the ball is in the opposite half the players should be in the wide zone (1 or 4); however, when the defending team intercepts the ball, the players may run into one of the central zones. For example, in figure 9.4, when white 4 intercepts the ball, he can play toward zone 3, setting up an attack.

Special rules

After a score, the direction of attack switches.

Scoring

The teams score by hitting the cones placed on the opposing team's goal line.

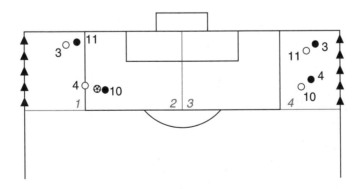

Figure 9.4 Cone scoring.

Variations

1. The ball may not be played back into one's own half of the pitch.
2. The players on the defending team cannot be closed down when intercepting the ball after getting possession of the ball in the central zone.
3. Only one attacking player and one defender are allowed in the central zone at one time (the width of the wide zones may be increased).
4. 3 and 4 must mark 10 and 11 as appropriate.
5. Play as in variation 1, but add that one of the defenders may be positioned in the opposition's half of the field; however, this player can take a maximum of two touches after coming into contact with the ball. Each team may add an extra defender and attacker.

Hints for instruction

In this drill the emphasis is on the decoy player's options for creating space for her teammates to use, and for getting free herself (running speed).

The drill also focuses on the timing between the decoy players and relative to the player with the ball. The decoy player will often make his run too early into the central zone, which limits his available space when he receives the ball. If the defenders choose not to go forward on the pitch, thereby making it more difficult to train toward the aims of decoy runs, you can increase the number of cones or implement variation 4. If it is too difficult for the attacking players to establish scoring opportunities, give each team an extra attacker.

In variation 1 the decoy player's options decrease, and the coach may wish to emphasize the decoy player's judgment when receiving the ball with a marker close behind her.

Variation 2 increases the number of through passes, allowing the coach to analyze the timing of the pass from the player with the ball. A quick pass increases the chances that one of the decoy players will receive the ball in a free position.

In variation 3 the two attackers must get used to being aware of each other's positions and assessing which of them should make the decoy run. The variation simplifies the situation for the attackers, and therefore it may also be tried out early on, when the players can have difficulties surveying the game.

Variation 5 focuses on the teamwork between the player with the ball and the decoy player. The player with the ball must, among other things, assess whether the decoy player can be used as a wall.

Keywords

Decoy player: running speed, receiving the ball

Player with the ball: assessment

Attacker Focus

Pitch

About half the pitch, with three zones—a central zone (2), and attacking/defending zones (1 and 3); two full-size goals

Players

16—7-v-7 and a goalkeeper on each team. Two players from each team are decoy players (10 and 11).

Description

Normal play, but the ball can be played in the attacking zone only if either 10 or 11 have touched the ball in the central zone. 10 and 11 will have to judge when to run into the central zone.

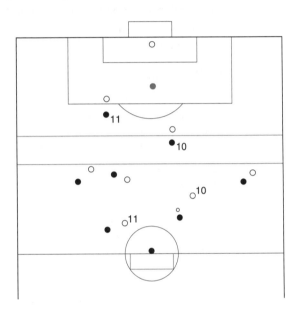

Figure 9.5 Attacker focus.

Special rules

10 and 11 must remain in the attacking zone when the opposition has possession of the ball (see figure 9.5). Only 10 and 11 may touch the ball in the central zone, and they have a maximum of three touches when in contact with the ball.

Scoring

As normal

Variations

1. On receiving the ball, 10 and 11 must pass with the first touch.
2. 10 and 11 are marked. The marking players may touch the ball in the central zone. 10 and 11 have an infinite number of touches.
3. All players are allowed everywhere and may make the decoy run, but the decoy player must come from the attacking zone.
4. It is not necessary that the decoy player touch the ball before it may be played into the attacking zone; however, the ball cannot be dribbled into the central zone.

Hints for instruction

The aim with this drill is for 10 and 11 to comprehend the value of making runs toward their own defense. The drill should also accustom the players to using a decoy player.

In variation 1 the decoy player is forced to orient herself before making her run toward the ball. Variation 2 increases the demands on the decoy players. Variation 3 forces the players to maintain awareness of the movements of their teammates and judge the appropriate moment for making a decoy run. Depth in the attack needs to be created before a decoy run can be advantageous.

In variation 4 the player with the ball must assess the situation when a teammate makes a decoy run. Should the pass go to the decoy player, or should the ball be played to another team member who can use the space that the decoy player's run has created?

Keywords

Decoy player: running speed, receiving the ball

Player with the ball: assessment

Specific Warm-Up Drills for Practicing Decoy Runs

Relay Drill

Players

4

Description

2 runs toward 1, who passes to 2, who plays the ball back with his first touch, after which 2 runs behind 4. Subsequently, 3 runs toward 1, who passes to 3, and so on (9.6a).

2 makes a run toward 1, who passes to 2, who turns and dribbles back when 3 takes over the ball. Meanwhile, 1 has started a run toward 3, who passes to 1, who turns and dribbles back for 4 to take over the ball, and so on (9.6b).

2 runs toward 1, who passes to 2, who plays a one-touch ball back and then runs behind 3. Meanwhile, 1 plays a long ball to 3, who, after controlling it, passes to 1, who has made a run toward 3. 1 passes with one touch to 3, after which she runs behind 4. In the meantime, 3 plays a long pass to 4, who, after controlling the ball, passes, and so on (9.6c).

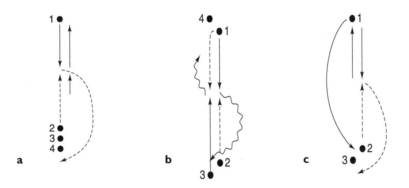

Figure 9.6 Relay drill.

Center Players

Players

6, 4 of whom have a ball

Description

Two players (decoy players) are positioned within a circle, such as the center circle. The rest of the players, each with a ball, are positioned approximately 15 meters from the circle. The decoy players take turns running toward one of the players outside the circle. This player passes to the decoy player, who, while outside of the circle, passes the ball back with his first touch. Every time the decoy players make a pass, they head toward the center of the circle (see figure 9.7). To encourage a high level of activity, introduce a competition: which pair of decoy players can complete the most passes (outside the circle) within a set time?

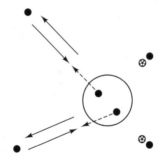

Figure 9.7   Center players.

Playing From Zone to Zone

Pitch

About a third of the pitch, with two wide zones (1 and 3) and a central zone (2)

Players

12—6-v-6

Description

Half the players on each team are positioned in one of the wide zones, and the other half are in the other. The teams score points by playing the ball from one wide zone to the other or to the central zone four times in a row, without the opposition gaining possession of the ball. A pass to the central zone is allowed only if the player receiving the ball was outside the central zone when the initial pass was made. See figure 9.8.

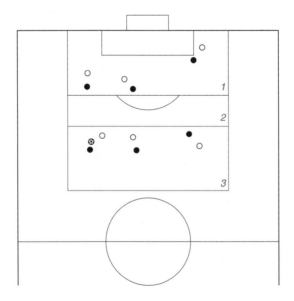

Figure 9.8 Playing from zone to zone.

CHAPTER 10

Combination Drills

Combination drills can be useful in easing the transition from specialized training of an attacking principle to using it during a match.

Principle

Use attacking principles in game-related situations.

Usage

Having practiced the various attacking principles, the players have gained a basic understanding that they must now try to incorporate into a match. The players may encounter difficulties in using this knowledge because in a game on a full-size pitch, it can be difficult to perceive and assess when to use an attacking principle. Combination drills can be useful in easing the transition from specialized training of an attacking principle to employing it during a match. Combination drills use a game situation as a basis; however, because fewer players are involved than in an actual game, the situation becomes clearer.

Aim

To ease the transition from training in specific attacking principles to using them during matches.

General Description and Hints for Instruction

In the individual situations that occur during a combination drill, the players must judge the appropriate action. It is the coach's task to guide the players, question their actions, and provide opportunities. The coach may stop the game, for example, if the players have misunderstood the performance of an attacking principle, or if some players cannot see and utilize opportunities created by teammates using an attacking principle. It is important, however, that the players learn from their own experiences in the beginning and that play is not interrupted too soon. In every drill we have outlined certain options for the attacking players. The coach can use these to guide the players so that they use the full range of attacking principles rather than using the same principle all the time. New situations will always arise where the players must again judge whether it will be possible and effective to use an attacking principle.

In the drills, the defending team should, on winning the ball, try to play the ball into the center circle with a high pass, using no more than five touches. Depending on the need, one or more players can be left out of or added into the drills.

Combination Drill 1

The drill consists of three match situations. Each one involves two strikers (10 and 11), marked by two opposing players (3 and 4). In addition the drill includes one attacker and one defender (2 and 5), as well as a goalkeeper (1). The practice can be carried out using two teams of six players each and a goalkeeper. The teams alternate between parts 1, 2, and 3 of the drill.

Fullback Dribbles Along Sideline

A fullback (2) dribbles along the sideline toward a defender (5) (figure 10.1). What should the other members of the attacking team do?

Options

1. Both 10 and 11 head toward the center, creating space for 2 to dribble past her direct opponent (challenging).
2. 10 moves toward 2 (decoy run), perhaps to act as a wall pass player.

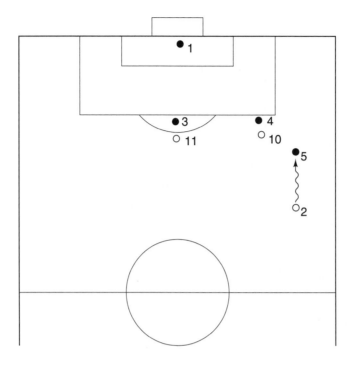

Figure 10.1   Fullback dribbles along sideline.

3. 10 moves toward the center and 11 runs out to the side line (crossover run), after which 11 can be played; or else 2 fakes a pass to 11 and then dribbles toward the center himself.

4. 2 dribbles inside, and either 10 or 11 moves behind 2 to overlap.

Midfielder Dribbles to Goal Line

A midfielder (7) dribbles to the goal line and is being closed down by the sweeper (6) (figure 10.2). What should the other members of the team do?

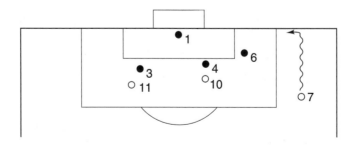

Figure 10.2   Midfielder dribbles to goal line.

Options

1. 10 and 11 complete a crossover, in which 11 runs toward the near post and 10 to the back post.
2. 7 beats 6 (challenging) and heads inside toward the goal, where 10 drops off to get a shot from inside the penalty area.
3. 10 or 11 fakes a forward run and runs diagonally back to gain the ball in a free position for a shot on goal.
4. 7 dribbles back and 10 or 11 runs out toward 7 to make a takeover or act as a wall pass player, so that 7 is able to dribble behind the defense.
5. Both 10 and 11 move slightly away from 7, then sprint toward 7. 10 runs to the near post and 11 to the center of the goal.

Midfielder Blocked at Goal Line

A midfielder (9) is not able to break through at the goal line and dribbles back followed by a defender (2) (figure 10.3). What can the other members of the team do?

Options

1. 11 heads back down the pitch and 10 runs toward 9 in the open space 11 has just created.
2. 10 or 11 overlaps on 9, when 9 dribbles back inside.
3. 10 or 11 makes, or fakes, a takeover with 9, so that one of them gets into a free position.
4. 11 acts as a wall pass player for 9, so that 9 can finish from outside of the penalty area (10 must move away to create space for 9).
5. 9 fakes a pass inside and then dribbles toward the goal line. 10 and 11 may wish to complete a crossover before the cross comes in from 9.

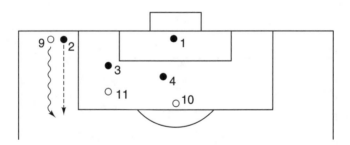

Figure 10.3 Midfielder blocked at goal line.

Combination Drill 2

This drill consists of three match situations. It is carried out with two teams, each made up of four players and a goalkeeper. The teams execute parts 1, 2, and 3 of the drill in succession.

Attacking Team

The attacking team consists of a fullback (2) and a striker (10), while the defending team is composed of a fullback (5) and a player (4) who marks 10, as well as a goalkeeper (1). 2 is dribbling down the line toward 5 (figure 10.4); what should 10 do?

Options

1. 10 moves back toward 2 (decoy run) and either acts as a wall pass player or receives the ball to continue dribbling.
2. 10 first moves toward 2 (decoy run) and then breaks inside, where she receives the ball.
3. 10 runs to the opposite side (creating space) so that 2 can dribble down the line (challenging).
4. 10 runs behind 5 (creating space), so that 2 can challenge 5 and cut inside to the center.
5. 2 dribbles inside so that 10 can overlap on 2

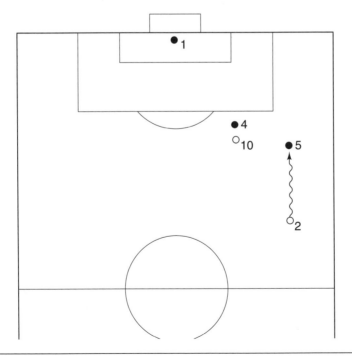

Figure 10.4 Attacking team.

Midfielders

Each team consists of two midfielders (attacking team, 7 and 9; defending team, 6 and 8) and a goalkeeper (1) (figure 10.5). 7 dribbles toward 6; what should 9 do?

Options

1. 9 acts as a wall pass player for 7.
2. 9 overlaps on 7.
3. 9 takes over the ball from 7.
4. 9 moves away from 7 (creating free space), so that 9 either becomes free or creates space so that 7 can challenge 6.

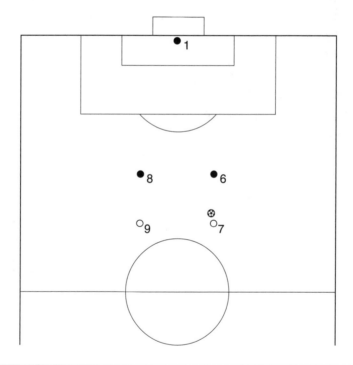

Figure 10.5   Midfielders.

Midfielder and Striker

The attacking team consists of a midfielder (9) and a striker (10), while the defending team has a sweeper (6), one player (4) who is marking 10, and a goalkeeper (1). 9 dribbles toward the goal (figure 10.6); what should 10 do?

Options

1. 10 acts as a wall pass player for 9.
2. 10 overlaps on 9 (overlap variation).
3. 10 completes a takeover with 9.
4. 10 heads away from the center (creating space) in such a way that he either becomes free or creates space for 9 to challenge 4.

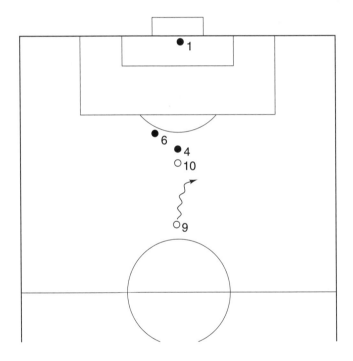

Figure 10.6 Midfielder and striker.

Combination Drill 3

On the attacking team there are two midfielders (7 and 9) and two strikers (10 and 11); while the defending team consists of one midfielder (8); two defenders (3 and 4), who mark 10 and 11; and a goalkeeper (1). The defensive midfielder (7) has possession of the ball near the center (figure 10.7); what should his teammates do?

Options

1. 10 moves toward 7 (decoy run). If 10's marker does not follow, 7 may pass to 10; otherwise 11 can move into the space created by 10 and receive the ball.

2. 7 and 9 make, or fake, a takeover close to 8; as a result, one of the players is freed with the ball.

3. 10 and 11 move out toward the wings (split run) so that 7 or 9 can dribble directly toward the goal.

4. 7 or 9 passes to 10 or 11, and 7 or 9 overlap.

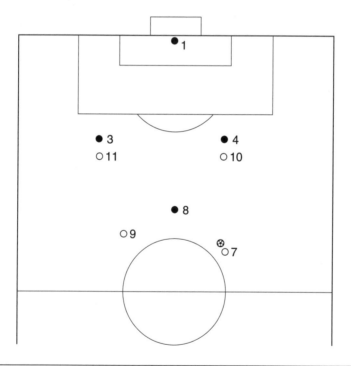

Figure 10.7   Defensive midfielder has possession of the ball.

5. 10 and 11 complete a crossover run, after which either 10 or 11 may receive the ball.

Variations

1. The defending team has a sweeper (6).

2. The attacking team has a fullback (2) and the defending team has one more midfielder (9).

3. The attacking team has one more fullback (5) and the defending team has one more midfielder (7, see figure 10.8).

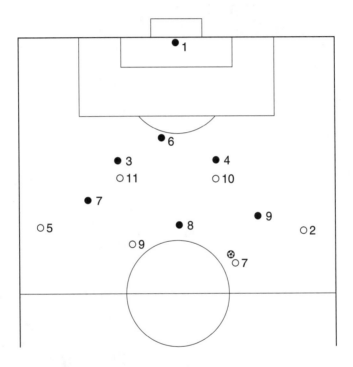

Figure 10.8 Variation with additional fullback and midfielder.

CHAPTER 11

Attacking Play: Buildup

Chapters 3 through 9 described the various attacking principles. In these chapters we focus on the team tactical conditions in which the players can use the attacking principles.

A soccer match is a constant alternation between *we have the ball* and *they have the ball*. Both attacking play and defensive play consist of different phases depending on where on the pitch the ball is, as illustrated in the model in figure 11.1. Attacking play consists of buildup in the defensive zone, of consolidating play in the midfield zone, and of breakthrough and finishing in the attacking zone. Defensive play depends on the team's style of play but usually means that a team should try to hinder the opposition's attempts at buildup in the defensive zone of the opposition, try to win the ball in the midfield zone, and prevent breaks or finishes in their own defensive zone. Within each area the players should be in a position to adapt quickly from attacking to defensive play and vice versa (*transition play*).

When *we have the ball*, "we" are all attackers; in other words, every single player should think along offensive lines: "How can I help to keep the ball and bring it forward?" Every team wants—consciously or subconsciously—to develop their own systems and playing styles. In our book *Soccer Systems and Strategies* (Human Kinetics 2000), the different systems

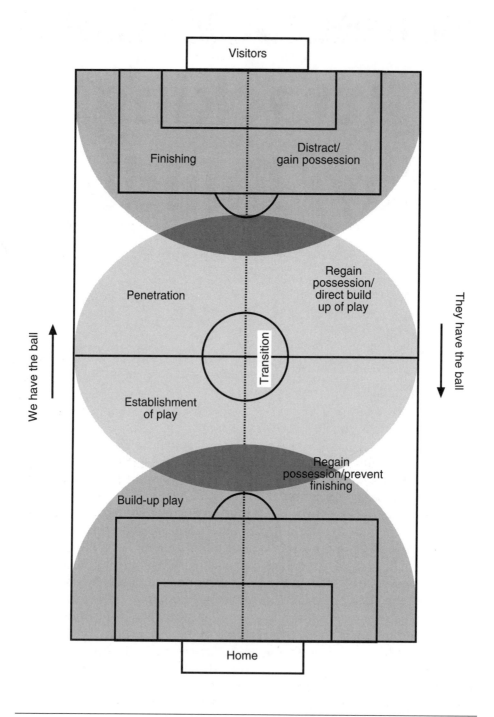

Figure 11.1 The different phases of offensive and defensive play.

and styles of play are discussed. Regardless of the choice of attacking form, every team will benefit from working with a wide range of tactical principles. We will deal with these in the coming chapters.

The chapter is divided into three sections:

1. The keeper's distribution
2. Width in the attack
3. Depth in the attack

The Keeper's Distribution

Principle

The goalkeeper sets the attacking play in motion by kicking or throwing the ball onto the pitch.

Usage

After receiving the ball, the goalkeeper is the first attacker, and he decides with his delivery where and how the buildup should start. Peter Schmeichel's goal throws are a good example of the way that a quick distribution can lend dynamism to a team. The players out on the pitch are equally responsible for the goalkeeper's distribution and should make themselves playable as in every other passing situation.

It can be beneficial for a team's stability in the buildup to rehearse basic situations in this phase. A practiced set of moves can, for example, bring the player who is most skillful on the ball into a propitious position to receive the ball, and thus give the team a good start in the subsequent buildup.

The choice of short or long goal kick or throw depends partly on the team's style of play and partly on what is appropriate in the given situation. With a short goal kick the team has a better chance of keeping possession of the ball, but the long goal kick can be very useful in certain situations, such as the following:

- When a quick counterattack can be set up, for example, when the number of strikers is equal to or greater than the number of opposition defenders. It is especially appropriate if there is a gap between the opposition's defensive and midfield lines (see figure 11.2).

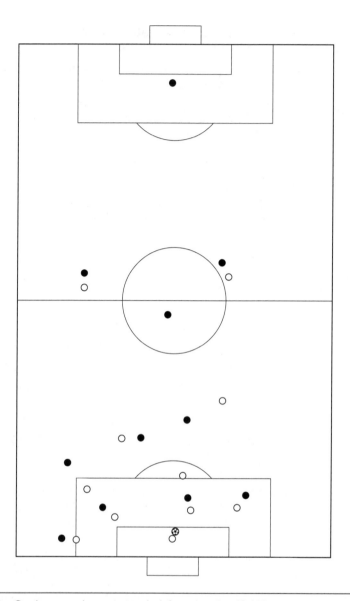

Figure 11.2   Gap between the opposition's defensive and midfield lines.

- When the team has at its disposal a player (target player) who is good at taking off and nudging the ball farther to an on-running teammate. This requires the goalkeeper to be in a position to hit the target player with a certain amount of precision.
- When the team is under continued pressure. With a long goal kick the players can move farther forward on the pitch and get a bit of breathing space.
- When the team wants to put the opposition under constant pressure.

Rule Changes

Since 1992 changes in the laws of the game have limited the goalkeeper's rights on back passes. The changes have brought a new and demanding function to the goalkeeper's game. The changes state the following:

An indirect free kick is awarded to the opposing team if a goalkeeper, inside his own penalty area, commits any of the following four offenses:

- Takes more than six seconds while controlling the ball with his hands before releasing it from his possession
- Touches the ball again with his hands after it has been released from his possession and has not touched any other player
- Touches the ball with his hands after it has been deliberately kicked to him by a teammate
- Touches the ball with his hands after he has received it directly from a throw-in taken by a teammate

These limitations mean that the goalkeeper, in her position close to the goal, is always in a pressured situation when the ball is played back to her. The rule changes also mean that the goalkeeper's time with the ball is substantially reduced.

General Description and Hints for Instruction

Main Points for Goalkeeper Distribution

Timing

The goalkeeper should judge when to distribute the ball. It can sometimes be advantageous to take the initiative and start play quickly, before the opposition have managed to position themselves appropriately (see also Counterattack on page 169 in chapter 13). In pressured situations it is often wise to allow plenty of time for the goal kick or throw, to slow the game down and give other members of the team time to organize themselves. The 2002 World Cup game between Sweden and Senegal provided an illustrative example of the role of a quick distribution. In extra time, the Swede Anders Svensson shot and hit the post. The ball was thrown out quickly by the Senegal goalkeeper, and Henri Kamara wriggled his way through to score a fabulous golden goal.

Delivery

A short or long delivery is decided partly according to the team's style of play and partly according to what is appropriate in the given situation.

Free space

The goalkeeper should look for and use free spaces. There will often be free spaces along the sidelines, especially on the side opposite to the one from which the ball came (transition play).

Communication

The goalkeeper should direct his teammates to take appropriate positions, letting the players know, among other things, the kind of distribution he wants.

Supporting player

During the play and after short goal kicks or throws, the goalkeeper should offer herself as a supporting player. She should, however, maintain an appropriate distance so that she has sufficient time and space to control a pass and kick the ball up the field when under pressure from the opposition. To increase safety in the ball-receiving phase, the pass back to the goalkeeper should preferably be outside the frame of the goal.

The goalkeeper essentially has three possible solutions on receiving the ball:

- Kicking the ball directly out over the sideline, if he is under severe pressure

- Playing a high and long ball forward on the pitch with a lifted pass or a volley

- Having controlled the direction of the ball, playing it to the side opposite the one from which he received it

In the drills for goalkeeper distribution we have used as a basis a team with four players at the back. By moving players between defense and midfield, you can easily adapt the drills to other playing systems, such as 3-5-2.

Goalkeeper Back Pass

Pitch

Half the pitch, divided into four zones (1–4) with two penalty areas; two full-size goals

Players

8—one defender (3), two attackers (9 and 10), and a goalkeeper (1) for each team

Special conditions

Player 3 from one team, together with 9 and 10 from the other, are all in one zone (zones 2 and 3) throughout the drill.

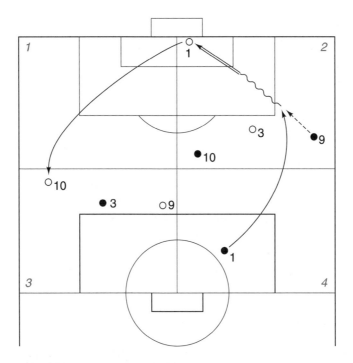

Figure 11.3   Goalkeeper back pass.

Description

One of the goalkeepers starts by throwing or kicking the ball out to 9 or 10. If 3 wins the ball, she passes to her own goalkeeper, who plays the ball forward to 9 or 10 in the opposite zone. See figure 11.3.

Special rules

The players may go into only one zone. In addition, 9 and 10 may not enter the penalty area before the ball is played into their zone. The goalkeeper has a maximum of three touches with the feet.

Scoring

As normal

Variations

1. 3 may pass to 9 and 10. 3 can take no more than three touches and can go anywhere in the penalty area.
2. When the goalkeeper has the ball, the players in zone 2 may run into zone 4. Similarly, the players in zone 3 can run into zone 1.
3. Introduce an extra defender to each team.

Hints for instruction

This drill works on the goalkeeper's play following a back pass and distribution with a long pass. The goalkeeper should constantly orient herself as to how her teammates are placed so that she can quickly control 3's pass and play the ball on. 3 should be aware that her pass to the goalkeeper will make it easier for the goalkeeper to decide what to do with the ball.

In variation 1, 3 should assess whether it is better to play the ball back to the keeper or to pass to 9 or 10.

In variation 2, by placing themselves appropriately, 9 and 10 can give the goalkeeper opportunities for both a short and a long delivery. On receiving the ball, the goalkeeper should quickly evaluate which player it is most appropriate to pass to.

Variation 3 increases the demand for precision from the goalkeeper and emphasizes the goalkeeper's role as a supporting player.

Keywords

Timing, delivery, free space, communication, supporting player

Goalkeeper Distribution

Pitch

Half the pitch, divided into two zones (1 and 2); one full-size goal and three small goals

Players

14—four defenders (2 and 5), two midfielders (6 and 7), one striker (10), and one goalkeeper (1) on the white team; two defenders, a midfielder, and three strikers on the black team

Description

Normal play

Special rules

On winning the ball the white team plays it back to the goalkeeper. The players can be in the penalty area only while the ball is there. White players 2 and 5 and black's three strikers are allowed only in zone 1. White 10 and the two defenders from the black team are restricted to zone 2. See figure 11.4.

Scoring

The black team scores as normal; the white team scores in three small goals on the halfway line.

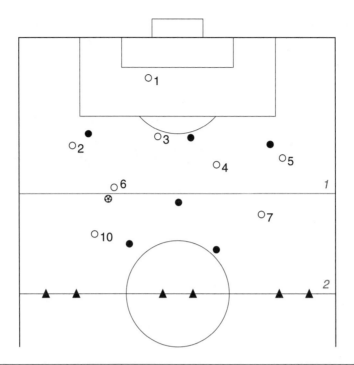

Figure 11.4   Goalkeeper distribution.

Variations

1. The players may enter the penalty area even if the ball is not there. The black team can score only from a cross into the penalty area.

2. In zone 1 the black team has a maximum of five passes before finishing.

3. The ball does not have to be played back to the keeper once it has been won.

Hints for instruction

This drill focuses on the assessments the goalkeeper should make when he receives the ball. Should he make his pass short and safe, or is there a chance that 10 can get free for a long pass? The goalkeeper's role as a supporting player is also underlined. The defenders should understand the possibilities and limitations involved with playing the ball to the keeper. The drill also emphasizes the team players, in particular the two midfielders, who should get a feel for how to make themselves playable for the goalkeeper.

Variation 1 sets the scene for a lot of high balls in the penalty area, which creates the opportunity for the goalkeeper to intervene or for the players to head the ball back to the goalkeeper.

With variation 2 the players are forced into quick finishes, thereby creating situations in which the goalkeeper must put the ball back into play. Variation 3 approaches a true game situation.

Keywords

Timing, delivery, free space, communication, supporting player

Goalkeeper Perception

Pitch

Around three-fifths of the pitch, divided into 3 zones (1–3); one full-size goal

Players

17—white team, four defenders (2–5), two midfielders (6 and 7), two strikers (9 and 10), and a goalkeeper (1); black team, three defenders, three midfielders, and two strikers

Description

Normal play, starting from the goalkeeper

Special rules

9 and 10 are restricted to zone 3, and the white team should have at least two players in zone 2 at all times (see figure 11.5).

Scoring

The black team scores as normal; the white team scores by dribbling the ball over the halfway line.

Variations

1. The white team scores by putting the ball over the halfway line following a headed pass from zone 1.
2. The white team passes from zone 1 to either 9 or 10, so as to get into zone 3.
3. A player who wins the ball plays it back to the goalkeeper. An opposing player may not attack the goalkeeper before the ball has been played into the penalty area, and before the player who wins the ball has been outside the penalty area. In other words, an opposing player cannot stay in the penalty area.

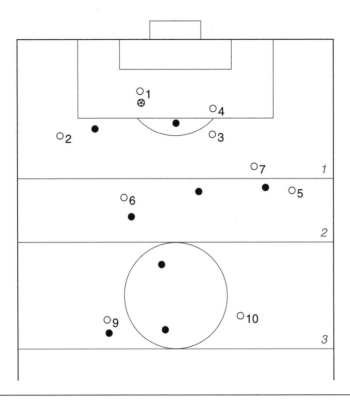

Figure 11.5   Goalkeeper perception.

Hints for instruction

This drill should create many situations where the white team is spread over a large area, which presents lots of opportunities for passing. On winning the ball the goalkeeper should get an overview of the positions of her teammates and opponents and then judge where to play the ball.

In variations 1 and 2 the emphasis is on the white team's use of a target player to quickly establish an attack. Variation 3 emphasizes the goalkeeper's role as a supporting player.

Keywords

Timing, delivery, free space, communication, supporting player

Goalkeeper Options

Pitch

Around three-quarters of the pitch, divided into two zones (1 and 2); two full-size goals

Players

16—6-v-6 plus a goalkeeper for each team, and two floaters (who play for the team in possession of the ball)

Description

Normal play

Special rules

Three players from each team and one floater should always be in zones 1 and 2 (see figure 11.6).

Scoring

As normal

Variations

1. The players on the team in possession of the ball may move anywhere on the pitch.
2. Introduce two extra players and omit the floaters, so the play is 4-v-4 in each zone.
3. After a player wins the ball, it is played back to the goalkeeper. An opposition player may not attack the goalkeeper until the ball has been played into the penalty area, and until the player who wins the ball has been out of the penalty area.

Hints for instruction

This drill focuses on the goalkeeper's and the defenders' distribution and play immediately after the ball has been won, when other members of the team are both close by and at a distance. The drill advocates short passing play after winning the ball, in that the team in possession of the ball has three extra players (floaters and an active goalkeeper).

Variation 1 increases the attackers' chances of being unmarked and thereby the chances of the goalkeeper making a long delivery. Variation 2 increases the demands on the players out on the pitch to make themselves playable. In variation 3 the focus is on back-pass situations where the goalkeeper is under pressure.

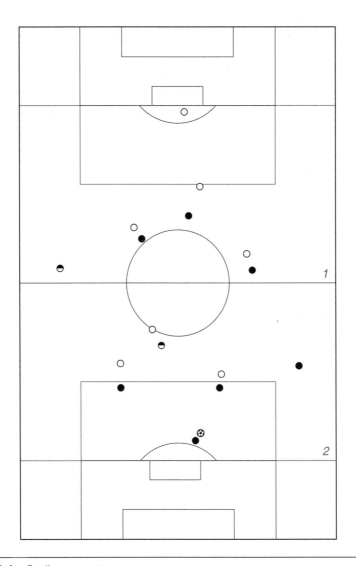

Figure 11.6   Goalkeeper options.

Keywords

Timing, delivery, free space, communication, supporting player

Specific Warm-Up Drills for Practicing Goalkeeper Distribution

Goalkeeper's Passing

Pitch

An area on the sidelines of about 10 by 30 meters

Players

8—6 attackers and 2 chasing players. 1 to 2 goalkeepers, alternating among attackers

Description

The attackers should be outside the marked-off area (see figure 11.7), and they can take a maximum of two touches on the ball. The chasing players should be inside the area. If one of the chasing players touches the ball, or if the ball gets more than a meter away from the area, the attacker who last touched the ball takes the place of one of the chasing players.

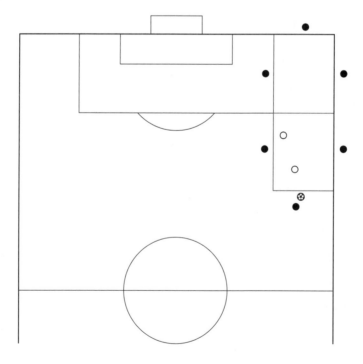

Figure 11.7   Goalkeeper's passing.

Target Game

Pitch

An extended penalty area

Players

10—4-v-4, plus two goalkeepers, who both play for the team in possession of the ball

Description

A 4-v-4 game is played in the penalty area, and the two goalkeepers are positioned in their respective areas between the penalty area and the sideline. A team scores points by playing the ball to one of the goalkeepers, who, with no more than two touches, passes with his foot to the other goalkeeper, who catches the ball and plays someone from the team in possession of the ball. See figure 11.8.

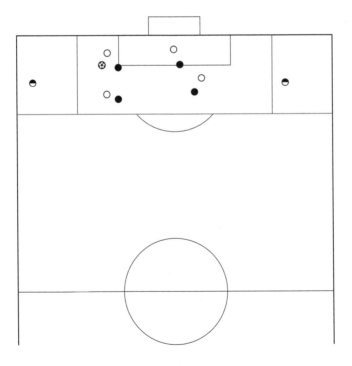

Figure 11.8   Target game.

Width in Attacking Play

Principle

Players position themselves on or move out toward the sidelines, thereby widening the team's playing area (see figure 11.9).

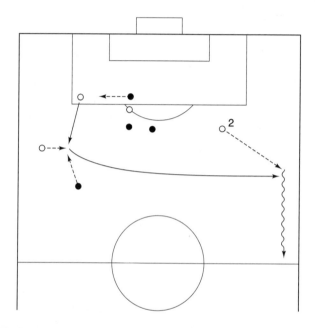

Figure 11.9   Players move toward sidelines.

Usage

The creation of width in a game is a vital tactical requirement for effective attacking play. The intention is partly to exploit free space at the sides of the pitch and partly to spread out the opposition players, thereby creating more space for buildup and breakthroughs in the center. To use the whole width of the pitch, a team must have wide players who remain near the sidelines. Ideally they should be technically proficient and willing to work within a small area. Marc Overmars of Barcelona is an example of a good wide player. One principle that can be successful is to transfer play over to one side, thereby pulling many players into this area, which then allows other members of the team to exploit the space on the opposite wing (weak-side attack). As the play shifts quickly from one side to the other, the player receiving the ball, say, a fullback, will often be able to penetrate deep into the opposition's half without meeting an opponent (see figure 11.10).

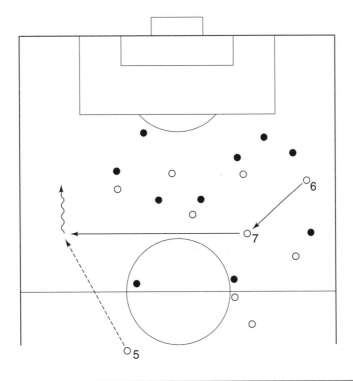

Figure 11.10 A tactic often used by Manchester United.

Manchester United often used this tactic in their very successful 1999 season, in which they won three major titles. The team established their buildup via the wings and then attempted to move in from one side. If a wing was closed off, the ball was played back to a constantly available supporting player (either Scholes or Keane), who would quickly pass the ball on with a long delivery to a forward-breaking player on the opposite wing.

Aims

1. To exploit free spaces at the sides of the pitch
2. To achieve more space in which to carry out attacking play

General Description and Hints for Instruction

In the transition from defense to attack, some players should move wide toward the sidelines to give the player with the ball passing options and to make the opposing team's defensive work more difficult (to move wide and spread their defense lines). Many teams make the mistake of simply sending all players up the pitch once the ball has been won.

Every player on a team should be aware of and should participate in creating width in buildup (overview, or perceiving the field and finding suitable areas to run to). While practicing the creation of width in the game, the players should become used to seeking width, thereby creating more playing space for themselves and their teammates (i.e., creating and exploiting free space). The overlap attacking principle (see page 53) is most successful when a team creates width in a game.

The coach should be aware that technical uncertainty can be a reason that a team does not use the pitch's width. Sometimes the wingers move in a few meters on the pitch, either to find more space in which to control the ball or because they are not certain that their teammates have the ability to pass over long distances.

Open to Space

Pitch

About half the pitch and a full-size goal

Players

7—two midfielders (6 and 8); two strikers (10 and 11); two defenders (3 and 4), who mark 10 and 11; and one goalkeeper (1)

Description

8 passes to 11, who plays the ball back to 8; 8 then passes to 10, who has broken across. 10 then passes back to 8, who plays 6, who has run out to the side into the free space created by 10. 6 dribbles to the goal line and passes to either 8, 10, or 11, who have all moved into the penalty area. See figure 11.11.

Variations

1. 8 and 11 play each other until 10 decides to run over toward 11.

2. Both 10 and 11 may create the free space at the side. After regaining the ball from 11, 8 plays across to 6, who plays 10, who passes back to 6. If 11 does not move across, 6 passes to 8 again, and so on, until either 10 or 11 moves across. If 11 runs across, 8 should exploit the free space and 6 should pass to 8; that is, the cross can come from either side, from either 6 or 8.

Hints for instruction

The object of the drill is to give the players an understanding of how, through switching play over to one side, they can create space at the

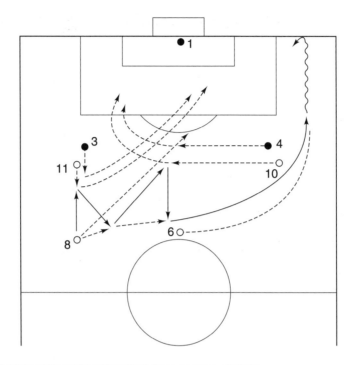

Figure 11.11 Open to space.

other side, and how this space can be exploited by another player
(6). 10 should run at a moderate speed to lure the marking player
with her, and 6 should hesitate in her forward run until 8 has the
ball for the second time. If they do not do this, 6 risks being too far
forward when the pass comes in from 8. This will make the pass more
difficult and means that 6's speed cannot be used, because 6 must
avoid running offside. In addition, a moderate starting position for 6
will increase the attacking team's chances of taking the opposition
by surprise.

Variations 1 and 2 give the players more choices and bring the drill
closer to a true match situation.

Keywords

Move wide, overview, create and exploit free space

Moving Spaces

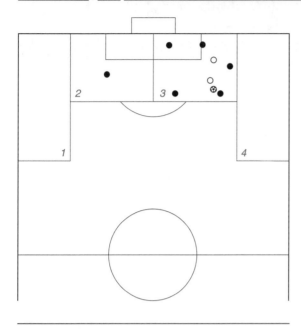

Figure 11.12 Moving spaces.

Pitch

Around a quarter of the pitch, divided into four zones (1–4)

Players

8—six attackers and two chasing players

Special conditions

The players are in pairs.

Description

The attackers pass to each other. If one of the chasing players touches the ball, he trades places with the player who made the error and his marker. The players may move into all the different zones. See figure 11.12.

Special rules

A player who has moved into another zone may not run back into her original zone until the ball has been passed into the new zone. The chasing players take an extra turn if the attackers have more than four zone switches without one of the chasing players touching the ball.

Variations

1. Introduce a limited number of touches—say, three.
2. Only one player is permitted in a zone where the ball is not—that is, a player who runs into a zone in which one player is already positioned must run into the next zone.

Hints for instruction

The game should help the players understand how they can increase the playing area by moving into a free space. Further, the players should get used to making themselves aware of their teammates' positions and to exploiting that a teammate is in a free position.

Variation 1 increases the demands on the players. In variation 2 the players should assess when it is appropriate to use the free spaces.

Keywords

Move wide, overview, create and exploit free space

Playing Wide

Pitch

Half the pitch

Players

14—7-v-7

Special conditions

Each team defends 10 cones positioned in two groups of 5 each and attacks the opponents' cones (see figure 11.13).

Description

Normal play

Scoring

The teams score by hitting one of the opposition's cones with the ball.

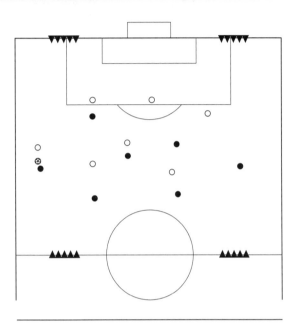

Figure 11.13   Playing wide.

Variations

1. A halfway line is positioned lengthwise. All players should be on the same side of the halfway line before a goal can be counted. If all of the defending team's players are not on the correct side, the goal counts double.

2. Carry out the drill with three lengthwise zones and an extra set of goals (see figure 11.14). Goals count only if all players from the attacking team are in either the middle zone or the zone where the scoring takes place (all should be in the middle zone if the goal is scored there). The goal counts double if the defending players do not fulfill this condition.

3. Carry out the drill with four lengthwise zones. Each team should always have at least one player in each zone.

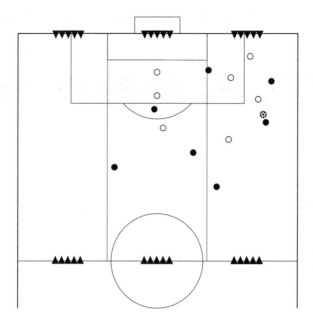

Figure 11.14 Three lengthwise zones and an extra set of goals.

Hints for instruction

The object of the game is to improve the players' ability to see and assess when they can create width in attacking play. In addition, the players should understand how to make use of width created in the game; that is, to have an eye for switching sides at the right moment. When the situation looks hopeless on one side, they can attempt something on the other wing. If the ball is constantly being dribbled across, the coach may wish to limit the number of touches (possibly only in the opposition's half of the field). The side switches are most effective when the ball is directly passed opposite. You may introduce one of the variations if the players tend to group together too much on their own half of the pitch.

Variations 1 and 2 focus primarily on the players' ability to assess when to create width in the game. Variation 3 aims at the players' understanding of how to exploit width.

Keywords

Move wide, overview, create and exploit free space

Zone Regulation

Pitch

Around three-quarters of the pitch, with a central zone that is divided into a middle area and two wide zones (see figure 11.15); two full-size goals

Players

18—8-v-8 and a goalkeeper for each team

Description

Normal play

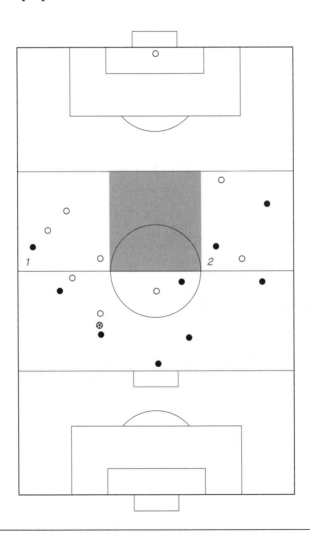

Figure 11.15   Zone regulation.

Special rule

No players may enter the middle area.

Scoring

As normal

Variations

1. For a goal to count, the ball must have been played in both wide areas during the attack.
2. If the ball is won in the defensive area, it must be played over the middle zone (i.e., from one wide zone to the other) before a goal can be scored.
3. The players may enter the middle area, but they may not touch the ball there. Otherwise, play continues as in variation 2.

Hints for instruction

In this drill the players get used to moving wide toward the sidelines at the beginning of an attack. They should understand how to use width in the game.

In variations 1, 2, and 3, the players are forced to use both sides of the pitch. Immediately after arriving in one wide zone, the players on the team with the ball should look at the possibility of getting over into the other wide zone.

Keywords

Move wide, overview, create and exploit free space

Specific Warm-Up Drills for Practicing Width in Play

High Pass

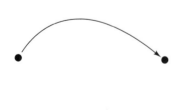

Figure 11.16   High pass.

Players

2

Description

The players pass long to each other (on the ground, in the air, or both). The player who receives the ball should direct it and accelerate for a couple of paces with the ball. See figure 11.16.

Fill the Zones

Pitch

About a third of the pitch, divided into four zones (1–4) plus a center zone

Players

12—6-v-6

Description

Normal play. No players are permitted in the center zone. The teams can have no more than three players in any one zone. A team scores by exchanging 10 passes within the team without the opposing team touching the ball. See figure 11.17.

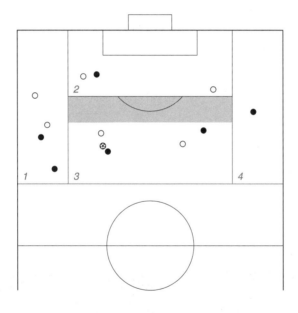

Figure 11.17 Fill the zones.

4-v-2 Double

Pitch

Two zones (1 and 2) with about 20 meters between them

Players

12—two groups of 4 attackers and 2 defenders (chasing the ball; see figure 11.18)

Description

Play 4-v-2 in the two zones, in one zone at a time. After 5 and within 10 deliveries (passes completed among the attacking teams), the ball should be played over into the opposite zone. The ball should be received without a challenge but within the zone. After the first touch, play resumes as 4-v-2. If during a pass the ball goes out of the zone, or if a chasing player wins the ball, the attacking player who last touched the ball switches with one of the chasing players.

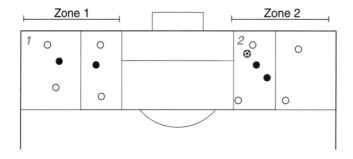

Figure 11.18   4-v-2 double.

10-v-5

Pitch

Two-fifths of the pitch

Players

15—three teams of five players each

Description

Play 10-v-5. The players have a maximum of three touches. If the ball is played out of the area, or if it is touched by a player from the defending team, the team of the player who made the error switches with the team that has won the ball (see figure 11.19). This exercise may be performed using two soccer balls.

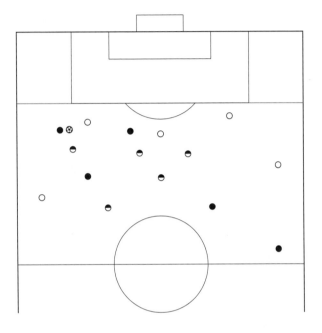

Figure 11.19   10-v-5.

Depth in Attacking Play

Principle
Players create depth in the game by running lengthwise away from the player in possession of the ball (see figure 11.20).

Usage

By creating depth in attacking play, a team spreads out the opposition over a larger area. This gives the team better playing space and more passing opportunities both forward and back. The offside rule, however, limits the chances of creating depth in attacking play in that the opposition's defense can reduce the playing area by pulling right back up the pitch. In these situations it can be appropriate to let one of the strikers move forward until he is level with the player farthest back on the opposing team, usually the sweeper. This player can be used as a target; he is the one to receive the ball when the defense plays it forward. For a detailed

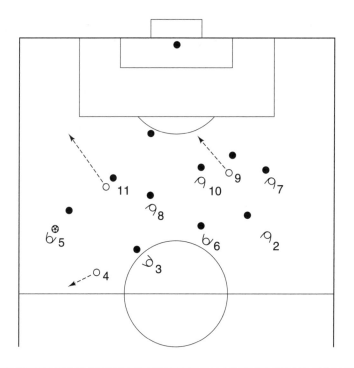

Figure 11.20   Creating depth in the game.

description of the way to use a target player, see our book *Soccer Systems and Strategies* (Human Kinetics 2000).

Some teams create depth in consolidation play with a player coming from the defense and breaking through the opposition's defensive line *(through run)*. A through run starts from the midfield area and is begun by a player who finds herself at a fair distance from the ball. The Dane Jon Dal Thomasson and the German international Michael Ballack are good examples of players who use through runs to great effect.

Depth in attacking play is also about unity between defense, midfield, and attack (see figure 11.21). One often sees a team "breaking in two"; that is, with too great a distance between the players who are farthest back and farthest forward, and the back players can therefore reach only the players in the midfield area. If this problem arises, the players farthest back should head farther up the pitch, and some of the players up front should move back toward their own goal.

Aims

1. To exploit free spaces
2. To find more space in which to carry out attacking play
3. To create passing opportunities forward and back

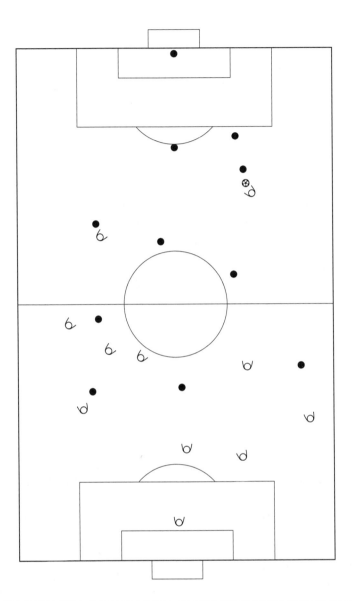

Figure 11.21   Team "breaking in two."

General Description and Hints for Instruction

Every player on a team should be involved in, and feel responsible for, the team having depth in attacking play. One or more of the players farthest back, particularly the sweeper and marking players, should move backward on the pitch and act as supporting players. The players farthest forward (the strikers) should head forward into free spaces and create depth at the front, while the midfielders should ensure that all the groups of players maintain contact.

By practicing the creation of depth in the game, the players will become accustomed to maintaining awareness of their fellow players' positions and will start noticing situations where it would be beneficial to break the formation with, say, a through run. The line of a through run depends on the player's position relative to the player in possession of the ball. The angle between the line of the run and the pass should ideally be between 45 and 90 degrees for the forward-running player to be able to use the pass. The player should make the break for the forward run preferably while the opponents' attention is focused on the ball. This moment occurs in particular when a ball is won or when the attacking play is about to halt. The through run requires the through-running player to make a long break and the player in possession of the ball to have a good view of the situation so that he can deliver at the right moment.

Meeting the Ball

Pitch

About a quarter of the pitch and a full-size goal

Players

6—one midfielder (8); two strikers (10 and 11); two defenders (3 and 4), who are marking 11 and 10; and a goalkeeper (1)

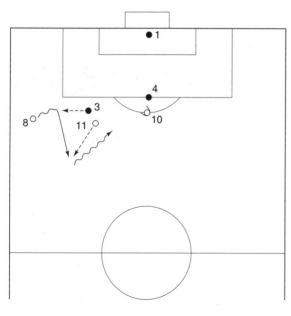

Figure 11.22 Meeting the ball.

Description

8 dribbles in from the side and is met by 3, who is marking 11. 11 runs down toward her own goal and receives the ball from 8. Following this, 11 can use 8 or 10 as a wall, or she can dribble toward the goal. See figure 11.22.

Special rules

Only 11 is allowed into the penalty area. The offside rule is in force.

Variations

1. Both 10 and 11 may receive the ball from 8. Only the player who receives the pass is allowed into the penalty area.

2. 8 is permitted to enter the penalty area. 3 can choose whether to challenge 8 or follow 11.

3. Add one more defender (a sweeper), who is restricted to the penalty area.

Hints for instruction

This drill makes the players realize that it can be appropriate to move back down the pitch. To stress this, halt the practice after 11 has run back and received the ball. Once 11 has taken the ball, 8 and 10 should take care to maintain the depth in the attacking play without moving into offside positions.

During variation 1 the emphasis is on the teamwork between 10 and 11; when one of them goes back, the other should remain forward.

In variation 2, 10 and 11 should see that, by moving back up the pitch, they have created space for other team players. 8, in addition, should assess whether it is appropriate to dribble or to play the ball.

Variation 3 should focus on the opportunities for creating depth forward.

Keywords

Supporting player, free space, awareness, through run

Support Play

Pitch

About a quarter of the pitch, divided into four zones (1–4)

Players

6—white team, one sweeper (4), one fullback (5), one midfield player (7), and one striker (10); black team, one defender (3), who marks 10, and one midfielder (8)

Description

Normal play. 4 starts off with the ball.

Special rules

4 is restricted to zone 1; 5 to zone 2; 7 and 8 to zones 1, 2, and 3; and 10 to zones 3 and 4. 3 can move at will. See figure 11.23.

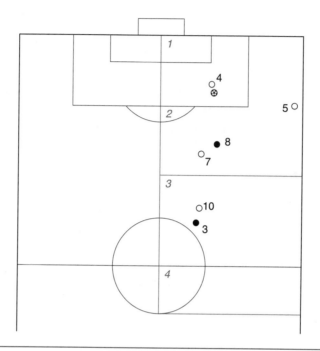

Figure 11.23 Support play.

Scoring

The white team scores by playing the ball to 10 in zone 4.

Variations

1. Add another black player (9), who can move freely over the whole pitch. 4 may also go into zone 2. Play is begun by 3 passing the ball down to 4. 7 can move freely.

2. Widen the playing area (see figure 11.24). A fullback (2), who may go only into zone 3, is added to the white team. 4 can move anywhere on the pitch.

3. Add one more black player. 5 and 2 are permitted into zones 2, 3, and 4.

Hints for instruction

This drill gives the players farthest back the experience of creating and exploiting depth during buildup. Before a player receives the ball, he should orient himself as to the positions of the other players. 4 should act as a support player. 7 should make himself available and on receiving the ball should assess the possibility of playing 10 in the depth.

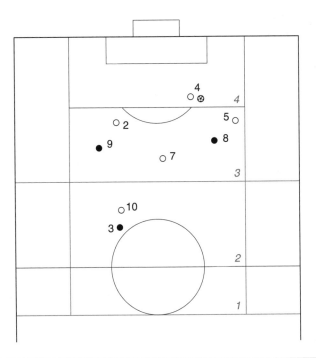

Figure 11.24   Support play—widened playing area.

With variation 1 pressure on the black team is increased. If black 9 challenges white 4, 5 and 7 should look for playable positions, and the white team should quickly play the ball forward to exploit their superior numbers.

During variation 2, emphasize that the passes require a certain amount of power to exploit the playing options in the depth. White 10 should assess on which side she should be positioned so as to create space for herself and for 7. The variation also gives 4 the opportunity for a through run.

Variation 3 increases the pressure on 2, 5, and 7, and it becomes more difficult for 10 to make himself playable. 2 and 5 can create passing options with diagonal runs.

Keywords

Supporting player, free space, awareness, through run

Coordinating Runs

Pitch

About a quarter of the pitch, divided into three zones—one penalty area (1), a midfield zone (2), and a wide zone (3); one full-size goal

Players

6—one midfielder (8), two strikers (10 and 11), two defenders (3 and 4), and a goalkeeper (1)

Description

Normal play

Special rules

No more than one of the attackers (8, 10, or 11) may be in zone 3 at one time. The defenders (3 and 4) are allowed only in the midfield zone. The attackers have a maximum of two touches in zone 1, after which they should look back to the midfield zone. The attackers can run into the penalty area only after dribbling or a wall pass. See figure 11.25.

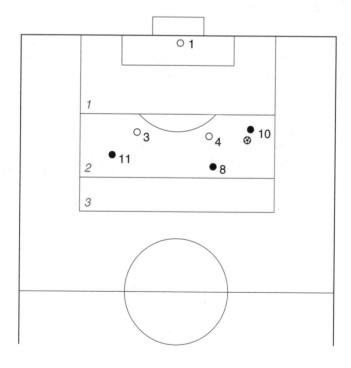

Figure 11.25 Coordinating runs.

Scoring

The attackers score as normal; the defenders score by passing to the goalkeeper, who plays a high ball into zone 3.

Variations

1. One defender may go into the wide zone. The attackers can have no more than two touches on the ball.
2. The midfield and wide zones become one zone. The offside rule is in force. The attackers may run into the penalty area if the ball is played into the area.
3. Introduce one more defender (a sweeper), who is restricted to the penalty area.

Hints for instruction

This drill gets the players used to being aware of their fellow players' positions and to moving in the direction of their own goal. When an attacker has received the ball in the wide zone, the remaining attacking players should try to help her, for example, by luring the defenders away or acting as wall pass players.

You can reduce the difficulty of the drill by increasing the size of the midfield and wide zones.

Variations 1 and 2 increase the need for the attacking players to be aware of their surroundings. During variation 3, emphasize the opportunities for creating depth forward.

Keywords

Supporting player, free space, awareness, through run

Three-Goal Game

Pitch

Half the pitch

Players

14—7-v-7

Special conditions

Each team defends and attacks three goals (see figure 11.26).

Description

Normal play

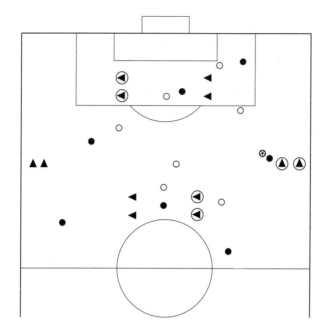

Figure 11.26   Three-goal game.

Special rule

The players may not run through the goals.

Scoring

A player scores by playing the ball through one of the opposition's goals to another member of the team.

Variations

1. The teams can score in all goals.
2. The teams can score only in the goals at the sidelines. The four "goalposts" in the middle denote a central zone. The ball can be played into the central zone only if it is played through one of the middle goals. If the ball is played into the central zone without meeting this condition, the opposing team is given a throw-in from the side.

Hints for instruction

The game focuses on improving the ability of the players to assess when they can create depth in attacking play. In addition, the players should understand how to use the depth that is created in attacking play, for example, by passing to a player who has come into a free position in the depth. The play may be stopped at the central goalposts and attention drawn to the running and playing options in the depth (to the goals on the sidelines).

Variation 1 increases the need for the players to orient themselves with regard to their teammates' and opponents' positions.

Variation 2 emphasizes the opportunities that arise from running into the attacking zone and from playing the ball from one's own defensive zone into the attacking zone.

Keywords

Supporting player, free space, awareness, through run

Awareness of Teammates

Pitch

About three-quarters of the pitch, divided into four zones; two full-size goals

Players

20—9-v-9, plus a goalkeeper on each team

Description

Normal play

Special rule

Each team should have at least one player in every zone (see figure 11.27).

Scoring

As normal

Variations

1. Increase the number of zones, for example, to six.
2. After winning the ball, a player should switch zones.

Hints for instruction

This drill accustoms players to being aware of their teammates' positions. Further, they should understand the need to ensure that depth exists in the attacking play.

Variation 1 increases the need for awareness. The players should not remain in the same zone constantly. Using variation 2 can help prevent this.

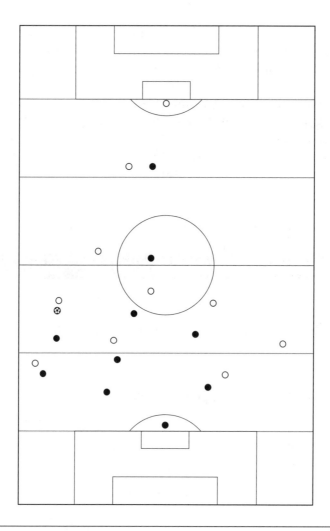

Figure 11.27 Awareness of teammates.

Keywords

Supporting player, free space, awareness, through run

Cohesion Play

Pitch

About three-quarters of the pitch, divided into four zones; two full-size goals

Players

18—8-v-8, plus a goalkeeper on each team

Description

Normal play

Special rule

The players must remain in two consecutive zones (excluding the goalkeeper). See figure 11.28.

Scoring

As normal

Variations

1. Each team may have players in no more than three consecutive zones.

2. Increase the num-ber of zones, for example, to six.

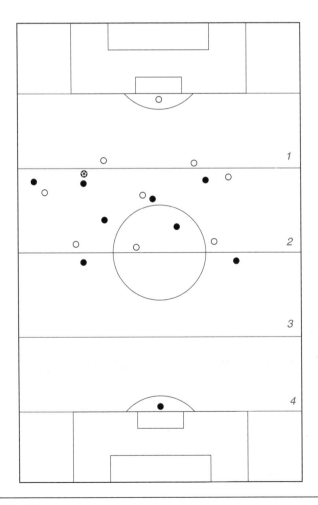

Figure 11.28   Cohesion play.

Hints for instruction

When the players work on creating depth in the game, at times there will be too great a distance between the team's defensive, midfield, and attacking units. This drill makes the players aware of teammates' positions and accustoms them to ensuring cohesion between the units. The drill also works on the transitional phase from defense to attack and vice versa, in that following winning or losing the ball, all players are quickly forced to participate in attacking or defensive play. This is particularly noticeable in variation 2.

Introduce variation 1 if the players have difficulty making the transition from one zone to the next.

This drill is organized along the same lines as Awareness of Teammates on page 151, and it can be appropriate to use it as an extension of that drill.

Keywords

Supporting player, free space, awareness, through run

Specific Warm-Up Drill for Practicing Depth in Attacking Play

Square Passing

Pitch

Square grid with a distance of about 25 meters between the two rows of cones.

Players

6

Description

2 runs diagonally and meets a pass from 1, carries it in her run until passing to 3, and then takes over 3's position. After her pass, 1 runs diagonally and takes her place behind 4, who runs diagonally and receives a pass from 3, and so on.

For additional warm-up drills, use those described in the section Width in Attacking Play in this chapter (see page 128).

CHAPTER 12

Possession: Change of Tempo

When a team keeps the ball patiently during attempts to create an opening until it can make a breakthrough, that is possession play. Many teams try to dominate the midfield and establish a consolidating play in the midfield zone. The midfield area, however, is heavily populated, and a great challenge lies in breaking the solid midfield block. One way to do this is by markedly changing the tempo.

Principle

A team changes speed in attacking play.

Usage

Several studies from Denmark and elsewhere have shown that soccer players at an elite level run quickly in a match far more often than non-elite players, but, conversely, that there is no particular difference in the final distance that both types of players run. These results underline the importance of both player and team being able to shift to a high tempo at frequent intervals.

During the 2002 World Cup we saw the worth of players who had the ability to take in the situation with a glance, as well as the physical resources, and set off dribbling at speed and thereby effect a takeover. The most eye-catching were the Brazilian Lucio's drives from the sweeper position (see figure 12.1), and the turbo attacks begun by England's Michael Owen and Denmark's Dennis Rommedal. As well as the initiative taken by running, a technical or tactical element, such as a wall pass, may signal to the other players that the tempo should be increased. It is often the team's playmaker who, through his initiative, sets up the change of tempo. Rui Costa of Milan and Zinedine Zidane of Real Madrid are fine examples of players who, through their own dribbling or by combining with another member of the team, get the whole attacking formation moving.

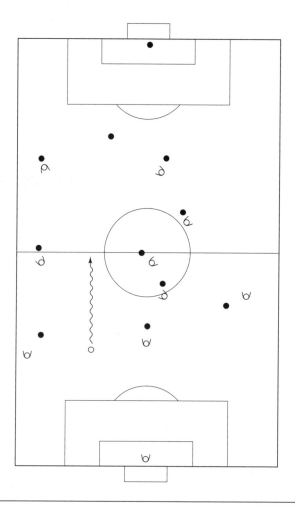

Figure 12.1 Drive from sweeper position.

Aims

1. To surprise and outplay opponents
2. To attack with high intensity at intervals during the game

General Description and Hints for Instruction

The timing of tempo changes can be directed by a player on the pitch or by the game's development. Winning the ball, for example, can be a signal to get an attack going, especially if the opposing team has been in the process of an elaborate buildup (see also Counterattack in chapter 13, page 169). Changes of tempo are especially important when a team uses the pressure style (see our book *Soccer Systems and Strategies*). A change of tempo can be concentrated within a few players, but the whole team must join in and support the players who start the change of tempo.

In this chapter's drills the players are forced to change speed in the game, which gives them an idea of what the change of speed is all about. The drills focus only a limited extent on when it is appropriate to change tempo and how long the individual phases should be maintained (duration). This knowledge comes from experience and depends to a high degree on the team's tactical strategies and abilities, including the players' physical capacities.

Change of Pace

Pitch

> About three-quarters of the pitch, divided into a midfield zone (2) and two wide zones (1 and 3); two full-size goals

Players

> 14—6-v-6, plus a goalkeeper on each team

Special condition

> All players except the goalkeeper start in the midfield zone.

Description

> The players should be based in the midfield zone, but they may run into a wide zone when the ball is played into that zone. Once the ball has been won in the wide zone—that is, when two players from the defending team have touched the ball twice in succession—play restarts in the midfield zone. See figure 12.2.

Special rule

The ball can be played into the attacking zone only following five passes in a row within the team.

Variations

1. Each team must have one player in the wide zones, even if the ball is in the midfield zone.
2. The players can move anywhere on the pitch, but on making contact with the ball in the midfield zone, each player should take at least four touches.

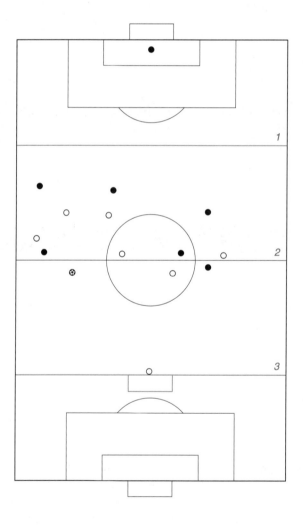

Figure 12.2 Change of pace.

Hints for instruction

This drill familiarizes the players with changing the speed of their runs. The game in the midfield zone should be measured; when the ball is played into an attacking zone, the play becomes aggressive. The players should be on the lookout for a good opportunity to change tempo, and everyone should participate when one or more players take the initiative.

In variation 1 the focus is on the change of tempo at the moment the ball is played forward to the target player in the attacking zone.

Variation 2 approaches a true game situation while continuing to emphasize the change of tempo, because the condition will in all probability slow the game down in the midfield zone.

Keywords

Timing, teamwork, duration

Acceleration Game

Pitch

About one-fifth of the pitch, divided into two zones (an extended penalty area)

Players

10—5-v-5

Special condition

All players start in the same zone.

Description

Normal play

Special rules

A team can play the ball across to the other zone only if all the team's players are in the zone from which the ball is played. See figure 12.3.

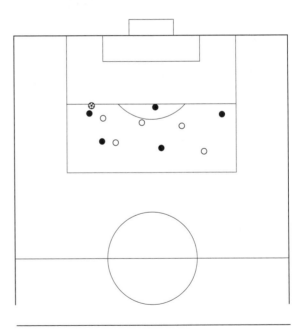

Figure 12.3 Acceleration game.

Scoring

The teams score points by playing the ball from one zone to the other three times in succession without the opposing team being able to play the ball between zones.

Variations

1. Four players on the team must touch the ball within one zone before the ball can be played into the other zone.
2. After the ball has been won, it is played over to the other zone within a limit of four touches by the team as a whole.
3. At least five passes must be exchanged within a team before the ball can be played to the other zone.

Hints for instruction

The players should understand how to carry out a change of tempo. When playing the ball between zones, the players should accelerate strongly so as to reach the new zone quickly; they should then slow the game down until a new opportunity to switch zones arises. The change in tempo will probably occur more often and the change in intensity will be more marked than in a match. On the other hand, the periods of change will not be as lengthy as in a match.

Variation 1 forces the teams to slow the game down when they come to a new zone, which is likely to make the change of tempo more obvious.

In variation 2 the intensity is increased in the play within the zones. Variation 3 teaches the players to be patient.

Keywords

Timing, teamwork, duration

High Tempo, Low Tempo

Pitch

Half the pitch, with a halfway line (see figure 12.4); two full-size goals

Players

14—6-v-6, plus a goalkeeper on each team

Description

Normal play

Special rules

On their own half of the pitch, the players have a maximum of two touches, and the team must have no more than five passes before the ball is played over the halfway line. The ball may not be played backward in one's own half.

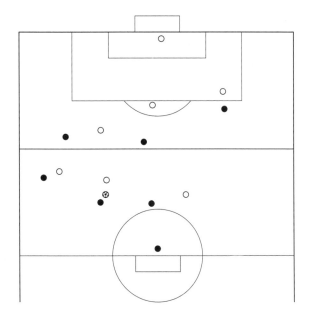

Figure 12.4 High tempo, low tempo.

Scoring

As normal

Variations

1. The special rules apply only in the opposition's half of the pitch.
2. The players should pass at least five times to each other (not to the player from whom they received the ball) in the opposition's half before they can finish.
3. Both teams always keep one player over the halfway line.

Hints for instruction

The teams play the ball quickly over onto the opposition's half of the pitch, where they slow the game down (change of tempo) from high tempo to low tempo. If the tempo is not high enough in their own half, make the conditions more severe—for example, no more than three passes before the ball is played over the halfway line.

In variation 1 the tempo shift is in the opposite direction—from low to high tempo. Variations 2 and 3 should increase the opportunities for achieving the desired shift in tempo.

Keywords

Timing, teamwork, duration

Intensity Demands

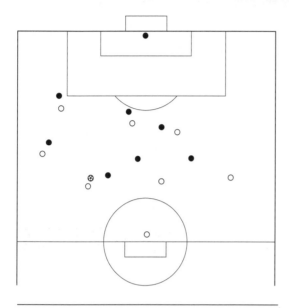

Figure 12.5 Intensity demands.

Pitch

Half the pitch and two full-size goals

Players

16—7-v-7, plus a goalkeeper for each team

Description

Normal play

Special rules

Each team alternates between two sets of rules. The conditions in set 1 are that the players touch the ball at least three times each time the ball is won, and the team exchanges at least 10 passes before finishing. In set 2 the team has a maximum of two touches and no more than 10 passes before finishing. One team plays according to set 1 while the other team plays to set 2. The teams switch rules about every three minutes. The offside rule is in force. See figure 12.5.

Scoring

As normal

Variations

1. The two teams play using the same set of rules simultaneously (switch about every three minutes between sets 1 and 2).
2. Set 1 is replaced by the following rule: The ball can be played over the halfway line only after five deliveries.
3. One player on the team using set 1 can, at a moment of the player's choosing, ignore the special rules; however, the initiated attack should result in a finish within one minute.

Hints for instruction

The players should understand the different demands posed during phases of moderate and high intensity. The team using set 1 should play with relative restraint, whereas the players on the team using set 2 should work with high intensity when in possession of the ball. The players have a great need for concentration in those moments when play is restrained.

Variations 1 and 2 can accustom the players to adapting themselves to new situations. Variation 3 focuses on timing a change of tempo.

Keywords

Timing, teamwork, duration

Specific Warm-Up Drills for Practicing Change of Tempo

Dribbling With Variation

Pitch

A penalty area

Players

1

Description

The player dribbles around the pitch, alternating between dribbling quickly and slowly, as illustrated in figure 12.6.

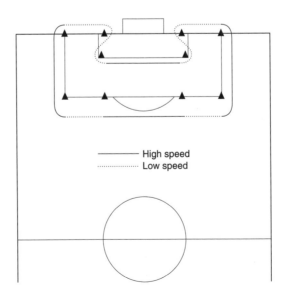

Figure 12.6 Dribbling with variation.

Crossover

Pitch

A penalty area

Players

10, half of whom have a ball

Description

The players dribble in the area, make eye contact with a player without a ball, and carry out takeovers. At a signal the players without a ball should try to win a ball. At a new signal the takeovers begin again. See figure 12.7.

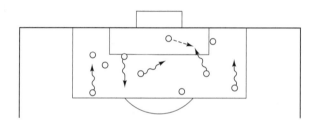

Figure 12.7 Crossover.

Two or Three Touches

Pitch

About a quarter of the pitch

Players

12—6-v-6

Description

Alternate between periods when players can take a minimum of three touches and periods when they can take a maximum of two touches. The two teams can have opposing rules; that is, one team's players have a minimum of three touches while the other team's players have a maximum of two touches. See figure 12.8.

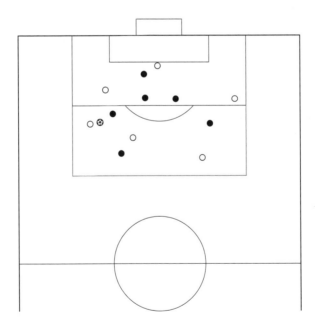

Figure 12.8 Two or three touches.

CHAPTER 13

Penetration and Finishing

The high point of a soccer match is seeing the ball in the back of the net. It is therefore worth turning our attention to finishing and how to increase its effectiveness. This chapter has four sections:

- Counterattack
- Breakthroughs
- Scoring opportunities outside the penalty box
- Scoring opportunities inside the penalty box
- Inclusive 1-v-1 against the goalkeeper

Counterattack

Principle

After winning the ball, the team in possession attacks the opposition's goal quickly and directly, in such a way that some opposing players are caught out on the wrong side of the ball (where they cannot contribute to any defensive work).

Usage

A counterattack exploits the idea that, following the loss of the ball, the opposing team's players have to adapt from attack to defense and are placed in unfamiliar positions. A counterattack can be an important tactical weapon, one that is especially effective when the opposing team has pushed many players forward. This situation occurs particularly during free kicks and corner kicks, where the goalkeeper, once he has won the ball, can start a counterattack with long, fast throw. For example, Peter Schmeichel's goal throws to Brian Laudrup on the Danish national team that won the European Championships, or to Ryan Giggs of Manchester United, have proved to be of the utmost effectiveness.

Many top soccer teams place great emphasis on counterattacks and use a defensive playing style in which many players are pulled back to their own defensive area. The opposing team often has difficulty pushing through and gaining finishing opportunities. Simultaneously, the players are positioned tightly by the defending team's goal, which gives the optimal conditions for a counterattack. Senegal's national team exploited this situation splendidly during the 2002 World Cup. A classic example came during the match against Denmark, when a Danish attacking player lost possession in his own defensive area, and after three passes and extremely fast runs made by three Senegal players, Diao scored an equalizer—the best counterattack move during the entire tournament.

Success in counterattack depends particularly on two player functions. A player must be able to bind together the defensive and attacking units *(linking player)* and, farther forward on the pitch, a striker must have a great ability to make breakthroughs. The linking player is normally positioned immediately in front of the defensive unit, and she should look for space as soon as the ball has been won. After receiving a pass she should bring the ball quickly over the midfield area and stay with the play right up to finishing. The striker should adapt her running work according to the path of the player with the ball, but on most occasions she should move indirectly backward on the pitch, and then at a high speed indirectly forward in the opposite direction *(V-run*; see figure 13.1); by doing so she becomes free to be played. England's Michael Owen is a player who fulfills this role outstandingly. When a counterattack is begun, at least two of the remaining players should set their course directly toward the opposition's penalty area, so that the pass in from the striker can find at least three recipients. Counterplay places great demands on the players' ability to judge a situation quickly and carry out the action.

Aims

1. To exploit that the opposition has many players forward on the pitch
2. To create situations in the opposition's half where the opponents are outnumbered

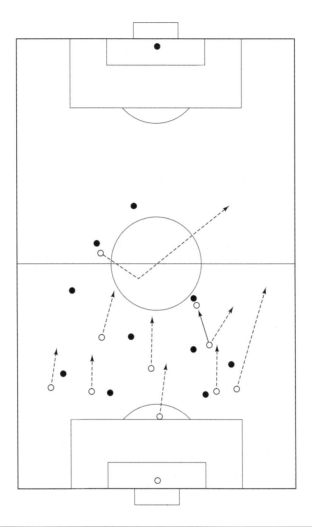

Figure 13.1   V-run.

General Description and Hints for Instruction

The counterattack can be divided into three phases. The first phase is winning the ball and passing quickly to a free player. In the second phase the ball is brought forward on the pitch, while the third phase takes place in the opposition's defensive zone, where the team should achieve a scoring opportunity and attempt a finish. In this section we will deal primarily with the first two phases; the patterns of movement in the third phase are discussed in the section Breakthrough (see page 201).

For a counterattack to be effective, the players must be in a position to adapt quickly from defense to attack, and they must accelerate immediately once the ball has been won (change of tempo). When the counterattack begins, the players who are forward should run away from the player with the ball to create free space or offer themselves to receive the ball (second phase). It is often appropriate to start the counterattack on the opposite side to that from which the ball has come.

Counterattack Drills

Following is a range of drills that introduce work with counterattacks. The drills assume that the goalkeeper starts off the counterattack; the players should bear in mind that the same principles of counterattacking apply when the ball is won out on the pitch.

Counterattack: First Phase

Pitch

> About a third of the pitch, with one full-size goal and two small goals

Players

> 7—black team, one midfielder (6) and two strikers (10 and 11); white team, three defenders (3, 4, and 7) plus a goalkeeper (1)

Description

> 6 dribbles to the goal line and plays the ball in to either 10 or 11. After the black team finishes or the white team wins the ball, the white team establishes a counterattack, which the black team defends. After a shot outside the goal, the goalkeeper starts the counterattack with another ball. The counterattack is finished when the black team wins the ball or when all three players are farther back on the pitch than the two goals. See figure 13.2.

Special rule

> 7 may not score.

Scoring

> The black team scores in the full-size goal; the white team scores by dribbling through one of the two smaller goals with the ball under control.

Variations

> 1. Scoring from a header counts double.
> 2. Add one extra black player, who marks white 7.

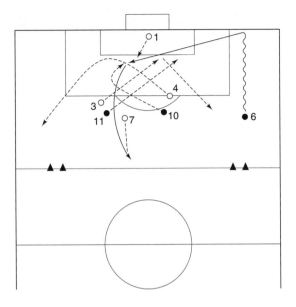

Figure 13.2   Counterattack: first phase.

3. Add one extra white player, who starts in the penalty area and tries to block the pass from black 6.

Hints for instruction

This drill introduces the first phase of counterattack. The instant the white team's players can sense that the goalkeeper is going for the ball, they should run outward and forward so that they quickly bring themselves into good positions to establish an attack. The goalkeeper's throw should be precise, so the players can take the ball at full speed. Instruct the black team's players to run back quickly so that the need for counterattack increases.

Variation 1 increases the goalkeeper's chances of getting hold of the ball, which leads to more counterattacking situations.

Variation 2 increases the need for 3, 4, and especially 7 to look forward quickly once the ball has been won.

Variation 3 gives the white team several playing opportunities but also puts strong demands on the players' awareness.

Keywords

Phase 1: adapt, change of tempo

Phase 2: create free space, middle stage

Changing Players

Pitch

Half the pitch, with a midfield zone and two full-size goals

Players

14—two teams of six, plus one goalkeeper for each team

Special conditions

Three players from each team play 3-v-3 while the other three from each team wait behind their own goal.

Description

Following a finish or loss of the ball, the players from the attacking team run out to the side and down behind their own goal, and the three resting players move in on the pitch and defend. These players must reach the midfield zone before they can touch the ball. See figure 13.3.

Scoring

As normal.

Variations

1. One of the players on the attacking team remains on the pitch after the ball has been lost, and only two new players run in.
2. One player from each team remains in the attacking zone. This player cannot score but must be passed to before the remaining players may enter the attacking zone.

Hints for instruction

In this drill the players become accustomed to adapting quickly from defense to attack. The players run at high speed after winning the ball, as this increases the chances of bypassing opponents because they may not defend until they have been in the midfield zone. The goalkeeper should understand the implications of distributing the ball quickly, and the throw should enable teammates to receive the ball on the run.

The players should pause between each performance of the drill so that they carry it out at a high level of intensity. Prolong the pause by increasing the number of players on each team.

In variation 1 the goalkeeper should maintain awareness of where the player who has remained behind turns up, and throw the ball to the opposite side. In variation 2 the emphasis is also on the second phase of counterattack. The players should develop an understanding of how they can use a target player (see page 141).

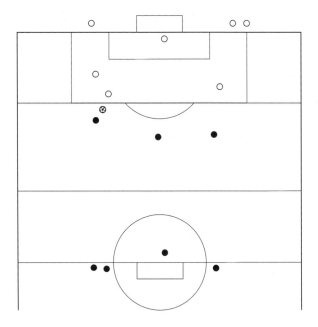

Figure 13.3   Changing players.

Keywords

> *Phase 1:* adapt, change of tempo
>
> *Phase 2:* create free space, middle stage

Time Constraint

Pitch

About three-quarters of the pitch, divided into two zones (1 and 2); one full-size goal and two small goals

Players

8—black team, one midfielder (6) and two strikers (10 and 11); white team, three defenders (2, 4, and 5), one midfielder (7), and a goal-keeper (1)

Description

After winning the ball, the white team has a maximum of 30 seconds to score. After the team finishes through the goal, or the ball goes out for a throw-in to the defending team, the goalkeeper starts with a throw (there should be extra soccer balls in the full-size goal).

Special rules

2 and 11 should remain in zone 1 at all times, whereas 5 and 10 must stay in zone 2. 7 may not go into the penalty area and may not score. After a goal or after the ball has been lost, 2, 4, and 5 must go into the penalty area before they can touch the ball. See figure 13.4.

Scoring

The attacking team scores in the full-size goal; the defending team scores in one of the two small goals.

Variations

1. 7 must touch the ball before the white team can score.
2. Add two additional players to each team (2 and 5 on the black team and 10 and 11 on the white team), and divide the pitch into four zones (1–4; see figure 13.5). The new players can go only into the new zones (3 and 4)—so there is one player from each team in every zone. The black team's 10 and 11 must not defend in zones 3 and 4. The white team can have no more than two players at a time in either zone 3 or zone 4. One-man offside comes into force. The white team has a maximum of one minute to effect a counterattack. The white team scores by dribbling over the halfway line with the ball under control.

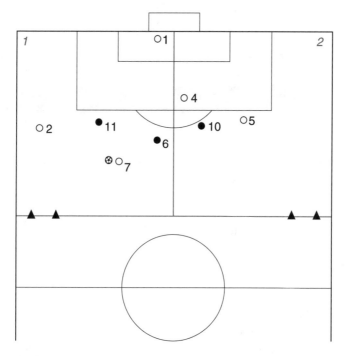

Figure 13.4 Time constraint.

3. Play as in variation 2, but zones 3 and 4 become one zone (three zones altogether) in which the players can move freely.

4. Play without zones.

Hints for instruction

This drill introduces the first phase of counterattack. The goalkeeper and the defenders become accustomed to looking around quickly and evaluating from which side to set the counterattack in motion.

It will often be appropriate to start the attack from the opposite side to where the black team has an extra player (6). After establishing a counterattack, the players should evaluate if it is worth switching attacking sides.

In variation 1, 7 should assess how he can make himself playable and take part in the counterattack.

Variation 2 illustrates the second phase of counterattack, which focuses especially on white 10's and 11's movements relative to the player in possession of the ball, and on the remaining players who are coming from the back. By their movements, 10 and 11 can create free space for their teammates.

Variation 3 places greater demands in terms of awareness on the players who are running from behind.

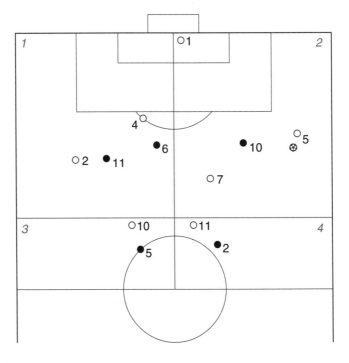

Figure 13.5 Time constraint variation.

Variation 4 approaches a true match situation. Players must carry out the counterattacks with high intensity, and it may be necessary to allow breaks in the action. Another option is to carry out the drill in the form of intervals, where the players in zones 1 and 2 switch out regularly with players who did not start out participating in the drill.

Keywords

Phase 1: adapt, change of tempo

Phase 2: create free space, middle stage

Counterattack Game

Pitch

The whole pitch, with three zones—two wide zones and a midfield zone (2); two full-size goals, positioned on opposite edges of zone 2, facing away from each other (see figure 13.6)

Players

18—8-v-8, plus a goalkeeper for each team

Description

Normal play

Scoring

As normal

Variations

1. All players must be in the wide zones (1 or 3) before a goal can be accepted.
2. Once the ball has been played into a wide zone (1 or 3), no player may run into the zone.
3. The players have a maximum of two touches in the midfield zone (2).
4. The ball can be passed no more than five times in the midfield zone (2).

Hints for instruction

This drill focuses primarily on the second phase of counterattack. The drill also accustoms the players to adapting swiftly from defense to attack, because a shot past goal can start a counterattack if the players quickly look for the ball. The drill also provides a chance to demonstrate what the players should do if a counterattack is not successful. When this is the case, the tempo is slowed and the players

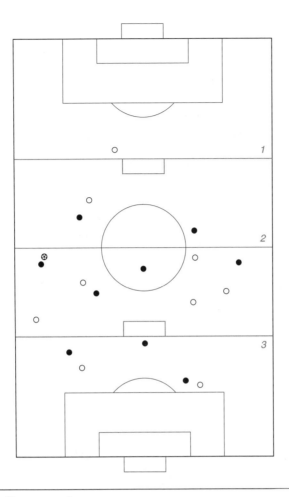

Figure 13.6   Counterattack game.

pass to each other until a finishing opportunity arises.

Variation 1 focuses on getting all players to take part in a counterattack. Variation 2 can be a way of increasing the speed of the counterattack, in that a quick attack should catch out a few opponents. Variations 3 and 4, as well as a combination of the two, also set the scene for fast counterattacks.

This drill can be physically demanding, and it may be necessary to introduce breaks to ensure that players carry out the counterattacks at a high level of intensity.

Keywords

Phase 1: adapt, change of tempo

Phase 2: create free space, middle stage

Specific Warm-Up Exercises for Practicing Counterattacks

Round the Cone

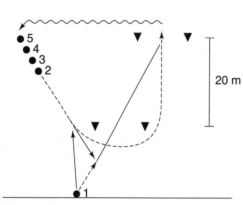

Figure 13.7 Round the cone.

20 m

Players

5

Description

1 passes to 2, who is running toward her, and 2 passes first back to 1. 2 rounds the cones and runs forward (V-run), where she receives a pass from 1. 2 reaches the ball before it passes a designated line. After this 1 passes to 3, who follows 2's example, and so on. See figure 13.7.

Receiving From the Goalie

Pitch

About a quarter of the pitch

Players

6—5, plus a goalkeeper

Description

1 plays a wall pass with 2, after which 1 plays a high ball to the goalkeeper before reaching the penalty area. Following this, 1 runs around the cones and receives a throw from the goalkeeper. 1 reaches the ball before the sideline and directs it on at full speed. After this, 3 does the same as 1. 2 is a permanent server. See figure 13.8.

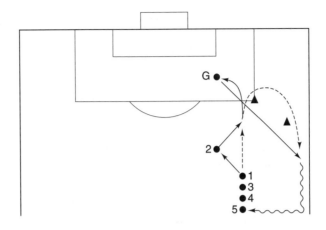

Figure 13.8   Receiving from the goalie.

Last Player

Pitch

About a fifth of the pitch, with two wide zones (1 and 3) and a midfield zone (2)

Players

6, one of whom is chasing the ball

Description

Play 4-v-1 (four against the chasing player) in zone 1, while one player is positioned in zone 3. At a signal the player in possession of the ball passes to zone 3, and the remaining players sprint to zone 3 (the passing player remains where he is). The game of 4-v-1 continues in zone 3, and the last player to arrive becomes the chasing player. At a new signal the ball is played back to zone 1, and play continues in the same way. See figure 13.9.

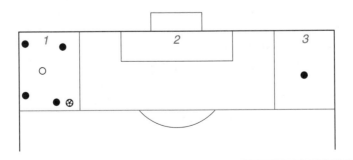

Figure 13.9   Last player.

Finishing Position: Scoring Opportunities Outside the Penalty Box

Logs recording the scoring patterns at various high-level tournaments give an idea of where goals are most often scored from. Table 13.1 provides information on goals scored in the final rounds of the World Cup from 1990 to 2002. The figures show that by far the majority of goals come from a finish inside the penalty area. This does not mean, however, that a finish should be attempted only when the ball is in the penalty area. Shots from outside the penalty also have their worth, not just because they can lead to a goal, but also because they can help to open up the opposition's defense and create space for finishes from within the penalty area.

This section describes the finish outside the penalty area in the form of long shots as well as breakthroughs and finishing in the penalty area. The latter section also deals with area-specific finishing following pass-ins, and situations where a player is in a 1-v-1 situation against the goalkeeper.

Finishing From Outside the Penalty Area

Principle

Players create free space for another member of the team who can finish from outside the penalty area (see table 13.1).

Usage

In modern elite soccer, a defensive style of play is reigning. The best way to open a compact defense is with finishes from outside the penalty area. If a team has one or more opportunists who are prepared to try a long shot, then the chances of breakthroughs increase, because the defenders are forced to move forward to cover.

In Danish soccer there are relatively few finishes from outside the penalty area, and this cannot be blamed exclusively on the players finding it technically difficult to master the long, powerful kick. It is also because not enough space is created for the players who do have a good kicking technique. This can best be illustrated by the so-called free kick experts who score many goals from free kicks but few from long shots. It is thus important that teammates create the necessary space for players who are strong shooters. This tactic was used to a great extent at Real Madrid to bring Roberto Carlos forward from the back.

Table 13.1 WORLD CUP BREAKDOWN OF GOALS SCORED 1990-2002

	1990 (52 matches)	1994 (52 matches)	1998 (64 matches)	2002 (64 matches)
Average number of goals	115 (2.21)	141 (2.71)	171 (2.67)	161 (2.52)
Finishing position (% of total scoring)				
Within the penalty area	80%	77%	78%	76%
Outside the penalty area	20%	23%	22%	24%
Headers (% of scoring)	24%	18%	18%	23%
Dead ball situations including penalties (% of scoring)	34%	25%	35%	48%

General Description and Hints for Instruction

Main Point for the Finishing Player

Utilize the Opportunity

The finishing player should be unhesitating; that is, after receiving the ball she takes only a short time to think, so that the defense has no chance to block the long shot (utilize the opportunity for a long shot).

Main Point for the Rest of the Team

Create Space

The teammates of the finishing player should either seek out the defenders to distract their attention or pull the defenders away from a possible finishing area (create the space for a long shot).

Two Against One

Pitch

About a third of the pitch and one full-size goal

Players

4—two attacking players (7 and 10), one defender (4), and a goalkeeper (1)

Description

7 dribbles and may pass to 10.

Special rules

7 and 10 should finish from outside the penalty area. From the moment 7 begins to dribble, 7 and 10 have no more than 30 seconds to finish the attack. No players may enter the penalty area. See figure 13.10.

Variations

1. The offside rule is in force.

2. One extra defender (6) stands 15 meters behind 7. 6 starts his run immediately after 7 has begun to dribble. 7 and 10 have one minute to finish the attack.

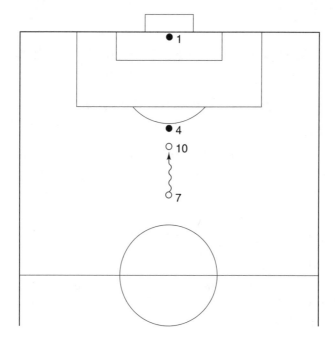

Figure 13.10   Two against one.

Hints for instruction

In this drill the emphasis is on teamwork between 7 and 10, which should result in one of the players getting into a situation where he has a free shot. Either 7 or 10 should move out toward the wing, so that 4 cannot mark them both at once. Attention can also be drawn to how 7's forward movement can lend power to the long shot.

Variation 1 makes things more difficult for 7 and 10. After passing to 10, if she does so, 7 should be prepared to watch her position with regard to offside. In variation 2 the pressure on 7 and 10 increases.

Keywords

Finishing player: utilize the opportunity

Other members of the team: create space

Creating Space for Finishing

Pitch

Half the pitch, with two penalty areas (see figure 13.11)

Players

12—5-v-5, plus a goalkeeper for each team

Description

As normal

Special rule

The players may not enter the penalty area.

Scoring

A shot on target counts for one point and a goal scored counts for three points.

Variations

1. Pick three players from each team who each have a maximum of two touches.
2. Two players from each team can be in the penalty areas at the same time. Within the penalty areas the finish must be made with a header unless the ball is coming from a save.

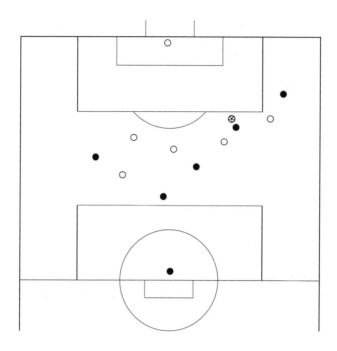

Figure 13.11 Creating space for finishing.

3. All players may enter the penalty areas, but players in the penalty areas may not leave while the attack lasts.

4. The players may go into and finish from the penalty areas. Scoring outside the penalty area counts for three points; scoring from within the penalty area counts for one point.

Hints for instruction

The team in possession of the ball should try to create space for finishing outside the penalty area. The drill also teaches decisiveness when a finishing opportunity is created.

In variation 1 the players whose touches on the ball are limited should primarily create space for the remaining players to finish. In variations 2 and 3 the players should understand that through their forward runs they can create space for other members of the team to finish.

In variation 3 the players also become accustomed to holding back and exploiting a shooting opportunity, if the ball is played back. Variation 4 approaches a true match situation, focusing continually on finishing outside the penalty area.

Keywords

Finishing player: utilize the opportunity

Other members of the team: create space

Table 13.2 GOALS IN THE GERMAN SEASON FROM 1992 TO 1993

Shots on goal per match		Scoring %	
Inside penalty kick area	Outside penalty kick area	Inside penalty kick area	Outside penalty kick area
17	16	85	15

Finishing Within the Penalty Area

Principle

A player can finish in the penalty area.

Usage

As tables 13.1 (see page 181) and 13.2 illustrate, the overwhelming majority of goals come from a finish within the penalty area. The players must therefore become accustomed to finishing in different situations and from different positions in the penalty area.

A shooting opportunity can be the result of an attack that has been played through when free space has been created for the finisher. It can also occur after a defensive error or after a return ball. The latter situation often arises unexpectedly, and the attacking players should therefore act decisively and sometimes imaginatively to perform successfully. A classic example came during a 2002 World Cup match when the Belgian attacker Mark Wilmots scored in a spectacular way with an overhead kick to give Belgium the lead against Japan.

In addition, an eye-popping shock came during Senegal-Uruguay when Diego Forlan (who also plays for Manchester United) trapped the ball on his chest and then thrashed home a dipping volley from 25 yards. Many goals can be scored from return balls in the penalty area, and it is wise to incorporate these situations into the team's tactical attacking possibilities. A most decisive goal was scored by Ronaldo in the 2002 World Cup final when Rivaldo shot and the German keeper, Oliver Kahn, could not hold the ball. Ronaldo came running in and put the ball in the net to take the lead, and later the trophy.

The most important element in soccer matches is the scoring of goals. There is, therefore, substantial pressure on the players who get on the end of finishes. This pressure is the reason that scoring percentages are higher in training than in matches. One way to reduce the pressure on the players is to get them used not only to looking at their own situation at the moment of finishing, but also to consider the situation as a whole, for example, to consider how difficult the game is for the goalkeeper.

General Description and Hints for Instruction

Training in finishes should give the players a certain confidence when scoring opportunities arise. The penalty area is often heavily populated, which means that players do not have very long to consider their finish. The coach should therefore aim at a certain automation in the finishers' actions, so that they will exploit the finishing opportunities effectively.

Main Points When Finishing in the Penalty Area

Precision

Players love to see the back of the net bulge, but many scoring chances are ruined through too much power being forced into the shot. In shooting, it often pays to prioritize precision higher than power.

Quick/surprising

Quick and surprising finishes in the penalty area, such as a toe tap in an unexpected situation, can have several advantages. The goalkeeper is unprepared and his view may be restricted. Moreover, the ball can brush a defender and change direction. On all of these occasions the goalkeeper has little time to react.

Return ball

Apart from the finishing player, the remaining attackers should be prepared for a return ball and, in every single finishing situation, should anticipate that the chance will arise. The nearest attacking player should always move toward the goalkeeper during finishes, to be on the spot.

The Cone Obstacles

Pitch

> One penalty area and a full-size goal

Players

> 3—one attacker (10), one goalkeeper (1), and one server (S)

Special conditions

> Place four cones in the penalty area (see diagram).

Description

S serves to 10 in front of one of the four cones. 10 rounds the cone and shoots first-time. 10 must finish on a possible return ball within 5 seconds. See figure 13.12.

Variations

1. 10 is told whether to shoot close to the goalkeeper or to the far or near post (the goalkeeper remains uninformed).
2. 10 is served a bouncing ball.
3. S serves outside the penalty area and 10 is facing the server (with back to the goal). 10 turns and finishes immediately.
4. Add a defender, who marks 10.

Hints for instruction

The drill focuses on 10's ability to assess the situation quickly and finish.

In variation 1, 10 gains experience with different types of shots. Variation 2 increases the demands on 10, and the coach can evaluate technical limitations. In variation 3, 10 should assess the goalkeeper's position as soon as she touches the ball. Variation 4 increases the need for 10 to assess the situation quickly.

Keywords

Precision, quick/surprising, return ball

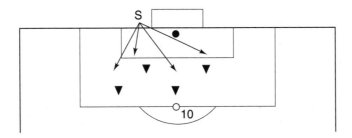

Figure 13.12   The cone obstacles.

Constant Finishing

Pitch

About a quarter of the pitch, with two full-size goals (see figure 13.13)

Players

14—two teams of six players each, who alternate playing 3-v-3; plus a goalkeeper for each team

Special conditions

Three players from each team are switched into play for one minute at a time.

Description

Normal play

Special rules

No corner kicks or throw-ins are allowed. If the ball goes out over the goal line or sidelines, it is put back into play by the goalkeeper for the side who should have the ball.

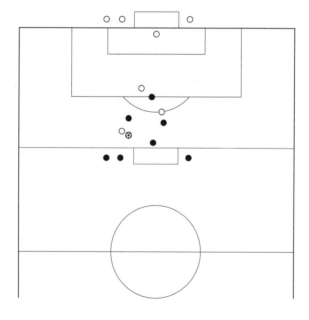

Figure 13.13 Constant finishing.

Scoring

As normal

Variations

1. The players have a maximum of two touches, and after winning the ball a team can make no more than five passes within the team before attempting a finish.
2. Play with marking defenders.
3. After a goal, the goalkeeper on the scoring team puts a new ball into play.

Hints for instruction

This drill accustoms the players to finishing from different positions under pressure. In addition, the players understand how they can create space for finishing.

Urge the players to finish often. If this does not happen, introduce variation 1. To maintain a high level of intensity, the goalkeeper should set the game in motion quickly if the ball goes out of play.

In variation 2 the pressure during the finishes will probably increase. During variation 3 the players should try to exploit that. Through quick backward runs toward their own goal, they can get free for a finish.

Keywords

Precision, quick/surprising, return ball

Breakaway

Pitch

About a third of the pitch, with two zones (an extended penalty area); two full-size goals (see figure 13.14)

Players

10—4-v-4, plus a goalkeeper for each team

Special condition

Each team has two players in each zone.

Description

Normal play

Special rules

No corner kicks or throw-ins are allowed. If the ball runs over the goal line or sidelines, it is put back into play by the goalkeeper of the team that should have the ball.

Scoring

As normal

Variations

1. The ball may not be played back into a player's own defensive zone.
2. Play with marking defenders.
3. The goalkeeper can pass only to the players in the attacking zone.

Hints for instruction

This drill teaches the attackers to accelerate to get into a free position, and to finish quickly under pressure.

Variation 1 increases the need for teamwork between the attacking players.

In variation 2 the pressure on the attackers when receiving the ball and finishing is increased.

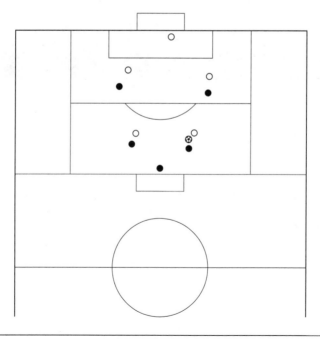

Figure 13.14 Breakaway.

Variation 3 may provide the attackers with some difficult balls and set greater demands on them with regard to creating and exploiting free space.

Keywords

Precision, quick/surprising, return ball

1-v-1 Against the Goalkeeper

Principle

A player challenges the goalkeeper to score.

Usage

To be in a 1-v-1 situation with the goalkeeper should be every attacker's dream, but this is not always the case. The sudden situation of being alone with the goalkeeper is often psychologically stressful for the attacker. Uncertainty perhaps takes over, causing the scoring chance to go unexploited. Sometimes, a lack of self-confidence can cause the player to stiffen when in a 1-v-1 with the goalkeeper. By observing certain basic principles in these situations, and through practice, a player will become confident with the situation, thus minimizing the uncertainty.

Main Points for Players in a 1-v-1 Against the Goalkeeper

Challenge

After breaking through, the attacker should, without hesitation, dribble directly toward the goalkeeper. The dribbling should preferably be a slow move, allowing the player to watch the goalkeeper's reactions.

Assessment

The player should assess whether to shoot straight at goal or dribble around the goalkeeper. The choice depends on the goalkeeper's position and reactions. The goalkeeper often comes out quickly toward the player to minimize the shooting angle. The shot or dribble should be made, if at all possible, when the goalkeeper is off balance or has just placed his weight on one leg. As a rule, this is immediately before the goalkeeper stops and prepares to make the save.

Shooting form

A passing shot should land just as the goalkeeper is on her way down to block the ball with her body. It may be placed right by the goalkeeper's feet, so her feet will be trapped when her center of gravity sinks as she attempts the save.

When an attacker breaks free on the wing, he can choose to pass inside to either the near post (short corner) or far post (long corner). Shots in the far corner are often easier for the goalkeeper to block, because he has more time to react and can dive with the ball. The goalkeeper will have greater problems saving shots at the near post, because the reaction time is shorter and the ball is closer to his center of gravity. Despite this, shots are most often made toward the far post, almost certainly because the opening at the far post is, as a rule, greater than that at the near post. In addition, the players often do not have the technique and the confidence to be able to place the ball in the smaller opening between the near post and the goalkeeper. Flemming Povlsen had the courage, and the technique, when he scored for Denmark in the near corner in the 1993 World Cup qualifying match against Spain.

If the finisher is a fair distance from the goalkeeper, who is off his line, a lob can be used. The lob can also be effective if the goalkeeper dives to the ground to block a shot. Many remember the Danish player Preben Elkjaer's splendid goal against Belgium at the 1984 European Championships to take the match to 3-2, when he lobbed the ball over Jean-Marie Paff, the diving Belgian goalkeeper. Players should be aware that the lob is technically very demanding.

Dribbling

Dribbling around the goalkeeper often demands a feint. To ensure a suitably large scoring angle, the attacker can move a little to one side and then move to the opposite side, out of the goalkeeper's reach. The attacking player should remember that the goalkeeper, by throwing herself, increases her reach.

Following is an drill in which players practice going 1-v-1 against the goalkeeper. For other drills, see the Breakthrough section (page 201), which also covers being alone with the goalkeeper.

1-v-1 With Goalie

Pitch

Half the pitch, with two penalty areas

Players

12—5-v-5, plus a goalkeeper for each team

Description

Normal play

Special rules

The players should be outside the penalty area; however, one player may dribble into the opposition's penalty area. See figure 13.15.

Scoring

As normal

Variations

1. The ball does not need to be dribbled into the penalty area. A player from the team in possession may run into the penalty area if the ball is passed in.
2. The defending team may have one player in its own penalty area if the opposing team has a player there.
3. All the players may run into the penalty areas if the ball is in the area.
4. The players may move anywhere on the pitch.

Hints for instruction

The idea of the drill is that attackers should break through and get in a 1-v-1 situation with the goalkeeper in ordinary playing situations. If the breakthrough player gets stuck in the penalty area and the situation becomes unnatural, a maximum time in the penalty area (e.g., 5 seconds) can be introduced, or variation 2 can be used.

Variation 1 should increase the number of breakthroughs. The coach can emphasize the timing of the pass to the breakthrough player. In variations 2 and 3, pressure increases on the breakthrough player. Variation 4 approaches a true game situation.

This drill develops along the same lines as Creating Space for Finishing on page 185 but this drill focuses on breakthrough and

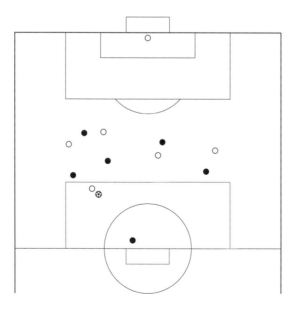

Figure 13.15   1-v-1 with goalie.

finishing in the penalty area. The players can benefit by carrying out one of the drills directly after the other.

Keywords

Breakthrough player: change of tempo, assessment

Other members of the team: create space, offer oneself

All players: challenge the goalkeeper, assessment, type of shot, dribbling

Hitting the Target

Pitch

A penalty area and a full-size goal

Special conditions

Place two cones on the goal line and six cones in the penalty area.

Players

1—one attacker (10)

Description

10 starts outside the penalty area by dribbling toward a cone. Once he has run around the cone, he finishes. See figure 13.16.

Scoring

10 scores by putting the ball between a cone and one of the goalposts.

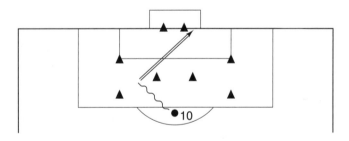

Figure 13.16 Hitting the target.

Variations

1. Introduce a goalkeeper (1). 10 must challenge the goalkeeper; scoring is as normal.
2. Add a defender (5), who positions herself at one of the corners of the penalty area. 10 plays the ball through 5's legs, and 5 then tries to prevent a goal.

Hints for instruction

This drill tests shooting accuracy. Pay special attention to 10's balance in the move before the finish. Players should practice finishing with both feet.

In variation 1, 10 should assess the goalkeeper's reactions before deciding how and where to shoot.

In variation 2, 10 should become accustomed to finishing under pressure. Urge 5 to challenge regularly.

Finishing From a Pass Into the Box

Principle

A player finishes following a cross.

Usage

Finishing situations often arise after crosses from the wings. The cross is useful because the defenders cannot see what is happening behind them, and they may have difficulty adapting. Further, the defenders are in a bad starting position to intervene—for example, against headers, their takeoff will not be as effective as that of the on-running attackers. The goalkeeper will encounter problems in covering the back post and simultaneously moving forward to the area by the near post. At a cross to the back post the goalkeeper is often forced to move backward or turn, and in doing so he risks missing something.

Team members must bring themselves into free positions on the wing. They can achieve this by exploiting different attacking principles as presented in previous chapters. In this section we will focus on the possibilities for the player who crosses the ball as well as those for the attacking players.

General Description and Hints for Instruction

Main Points for the Crossing Player

Passing position

The player crossing the ball into the area can choose to do so as early as around the edges of the penalty area (see figure 13.17). On most occasions a hard, flat, outward-curving ball placed between the defenders and the goalkeeper will be most effective. This type of ball is difficult for the defenders to block, and the pass has a good chance of reaching an attacker running onto the far post. The cross from the goal line can often cause problems for the defense, because the attackers can look toward the ball, whereas the defenders must run toward their own goal.

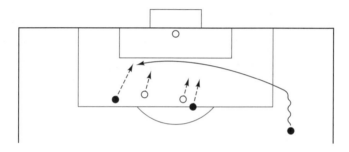

Figure 13.17   Passing position.

Awareness

The crossing player should look up to orient herself to her teammates' and opponents' positions. It is desirable, however, that the other team members run in predetermined paths (near and far posts) so that the player putting the ball in can concentrate on the cross when she is under pressure.

Passing

The cross can be played into different areas (see figure 13.18). The form the pass takes depends on where the ball needs to be played to.

Near Post

The pass should be strong, at head height, or gently curved so that the ball can be headed on or into the goal at the near post. If only a few players are in the penalty area, the ball may alternatively be passed hard and flat to a forward-breaking player who can tap the ball into the goal or possibly jump over it to confuse the defense.

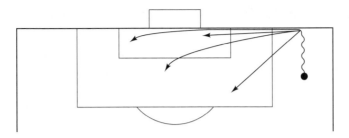

Figure 13.18   The cross played into different areas.

The Center and the Far Post

The path of the ball should be curved and heading away from the goalkeeper. A player best achieves this by taking the kick with the right foot on the right wing and the left foot on the left wing. To achieve spin, the player can also play the ball a little out toward the side before the kick.

The deep crosses should preferably be just far enough from the goalkeeper's reach that he becomes unsure of how far he should try to interfere (see figure 13.19). The far corner of the goal area is normally a good point for the crossing player to aim at. Before the pass lands, the other attacking team members in the area will often be so far from the goal area that the marking is slack.

Indirectly Backward

A pass indirectly backward to a teammate can be effective if many players have moved close to the goal. It can be exploited particularly in situations where the crossing player has the opportunity to break toward the goal along the back line.

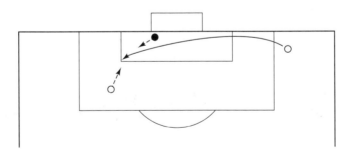

Figure 13.19   Deep crosses out of goalkeeper's reach.

Main Points for the Attackers in the Area

When to move

The attackers should adjust their runs in relation to the cross. They often break too soon, allowing the defenders to take up new defensive positions; this means that all players are standing still when the ball is received, and the chances of scoring are substantially reduced. The break should come at the moment the pass is taken.

Running paths

The attackers' running patterns should, as far as possible, be parallel with the route of the ball, so that the finisher runs onto the ball. If the player meets the ball at an angle, it will be more difficult both to time and to make the finish (see figure 13.20; player 2's direction of run is the best).

Teamwork

The attackers should work together and consciously seek different positions. One should break to the near post and one to the far post (see also crossover run, page 79). A third player should possibly make herself playable for a pass indirectly backward, while the remaining players seek alternative options in or immediately outside the penalty area.

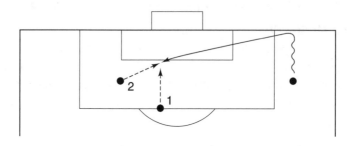

Figure 13.20   Running patterns parallel to ball's path.

Approach Runs

Pitch

About one-fifth of the pitch and one full-size goal

Players

3—one crossing player (2), one attacker (10), and one goalkeeper (1)

Special condition

10 starts outside the penalty area.

Description

2 dribbles to the goal line and passes in to 10, who attempts a finish. See figure 13.21.

Variations

1. Add one more attacker (11), who undertakes a crossover run with 10. 2 passes to either 10 or 11.
2. Introduce a defender, who may choose a position freely within the penalty area.
3. Add a defender and another attacker (7), who may not enter the penalty area. The game continues until the ball goes out of play, or until the goalkeeper has the ball.
4. Play as in variation 3, but 7 may enter the penalty area.

Hints for instruction

The drill focuses on when and how 2 passes, as well as on 10's timing relative to the cross.

Variation 1 teaches teamwork between 10 and 11. In variation 2 the need for 2's awareness increases. In variation 3, 2 should be aware of the option of playing the ball indirectly back to 7. Variation 4 approaches a true match situation. Focus attention on the teamwork between the three attacking players.

Keywords

Crossing player: passing position, awareness, delivery

Finishing players: timing of move, running path, teamwork

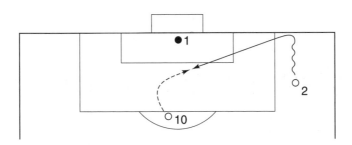

Figure 13.21 Approach runs.

Channel Space

Pitch

About a third of the pitch, with a halfway line and two wide zones (channels); two full-size goals

Players

18—two teams of six (players will play 3-v-3), plus two wingers and one goalkeeper for each team

Special conditions

The two wingers from each team play at all times; the three remaining players from each team are switched into play, one minute at a time. See figure 13.22.

Description

Normal play

Special rules

The wingers are restricted to the channels in the attacking zone. No other player may go into the channels. There are no corner kicks or throw-ins. If the ball runs out over the goal line or the sidelines, it is put back into play by the goalkeeper on the side that should have the ball.

Scoring

As normal

Variations

1. A goal may be scored only following a cross from the wingers. Alternatively, scoring from a cross from the wingers counts double.
2. The wingers may have no more than three touches on the ball, and the ball may not reach a standstill in the channels.
3. There is no halfway line in the channels, so the wingers can move anywhere within the channels.
4. Play without wingers. A player from the team with the ball may move out to the channels in the attacking zone.

Hints for instruction

The drill gets the players accustomed to seeking finishing positions at a cross from the wing.

Variation 1 can be used if there are too few crosses.

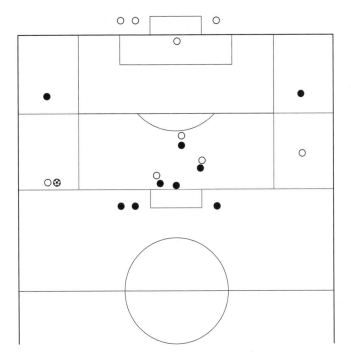

Figure 13.22   Channel space.

Variation 2 helps prevent the cross from becoming unnatural. The players therefore have more opportunity to time their approaches.

In variation 3 the pressure on the wingers increases, which also places greater timing demands on the players in the penalty area.

Variation 4 approaches a true game situation.

Breakthrough

Principle

A player breaks through the opposition's defensive line and gets within range of the goal.

Usage

When the players approach the opposition's penalty area, the playing area is narrowed. To break through, therefore, the attackers must often dribble or use some slick combination play, perhaps with first-touch passes or passes in depth. The players should quickly get an overview of their teammates' positions, so that they have an idea of where there is space for the next playing action. Filippo Inzaghi and Ronaldo are fine examples of players who can take in the field at a glance, which makes them unpredictable for a defense.

Figure 13.23 illustrates a playing situation where a breakthrough is created close by the goal. White 9 challenges the black defense by dribbling across, and just as one more black defender moves toward him, he passes in depth to white 10. White 10 has taken in the playing opportunity and receives the ball in a free position. Zidane, in particular, has a great ability to see and exploit such breakthrough opportunities. Far from all of his passes get through to another member of the team, but a great scoring chance arises when a pass is successful. In the finishing zone a team must allow itself to risk losing the ball by attempting passes that will create chances.

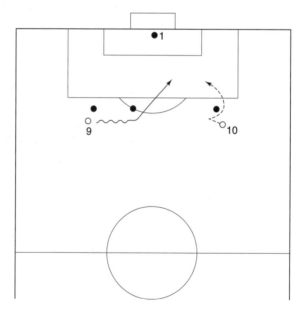

Figure 13.23 Breakthrough created close by the goal.

General Description and Hints for Instruction

Main Points for the Breakthrough Player

Change of tempo

To exploit the playing situation, the breakthrough player should run at a high speed.

Evaluation

If the breakthrough player has the ball, she should evaluate whether it is possible to undertake a breakthrough by dribbling or via a pass to another member of the team, for example, a wall pass. If the breakthrough player does not have the ball, she should choose to start her breakthrough at such a time that the player in possession of the ball can pass before the breakthrough player goes offside.

Purpose

The breakthrough should be purposeful to be effective. Often, a player who has broken through seems surprised to be free and hesitates, allowing a defender the opportunity to disrupt the finish.

Main Points for Other Members of the Team

Create space

The teammates of the breakthrough player should create space by heading away from an area that could be used for a breakthrough. The players can exploit that the defense's attention is directed toward the breakthrough player by getting into playable positions.

Show oneself

Some of the teammates can offer themselves as a wall pass partner for the breakthrough player.

Challenging

Pitch

About a third of the pitch and one full-size goal

Players

4—two attackers (7 and 10); one defender (4), who marks 10; and a goalkeeper (1)

Description

7 dribbles and may pass to 10 (see figure 13.24).

Special rules

4 may not enter the penalty area, and only one of the attackers may. 7 and 10 should finish from within the penalty area. From the point at which 7 begins to dribble, 7 and 10 have no longer than 20 seconds to finish off the attack.

Variations

1. The offside rule is in force.
2. 7 and 10 are told whether they should shoot or dribble past the goalkeeper (the goalkeeper remains uninformed).

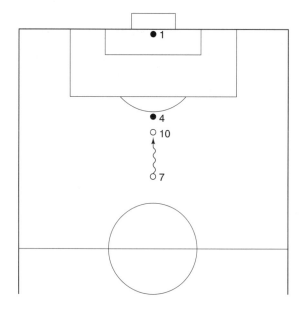

Figure 13.24 Challenging.

3. Add one more defender (6), who stands 15 meters behind 7. 6 starts his run immediately after 7 has begun dribbling. 7 and 10 have one minute to finish the attack.

Hints for instruction

The drill focuses on 7 and 10's evaluations of breakthrough opportunities, together with the teamwork between 7 and 10. Emphasize the opportunities for completing a wall pass.

Variation 1 can focus on the timing between 7 and 10. A pass into the penalty area should be played at the right time and with suitable power so that the attacker does not go offside and the goalkeeper cannot get hold of it.

In variation 2, 7 and 10 are forced to follow a predetermined course of action and thereby experience the opportunities and limitations of being in a 1-v-1 situation against the goalkeeper.

Variation 3 increases the need for mutual communication between 7 and 10; they must find quick solutions.

This drill develops along the same lines as figure 13.10 in Finishing Outside the Penalty Area on page 184, but in this case the emphasis is on breakthrough and finishing in the penalty area. The players can benefit by practicing one of these drills directly after the another.

This drill can also help players practice 1-v-1 situations against the goalkeeper (see page 192).

Keywords

Breakthrough player: change of tempo, assessment

Other members of the team: create space, offer oneself

All players: challenge the goalkeeper, assessment, type of shot, dribbling

Change of Tempo

Pitch

About a third of the pitch, divided into two zones (1 and 2), and one full-size goal

Players

6—three attackers, two defenders, and a goalkeeper

Description

The players are in zone 1; however, one of the attackers must dribble or direct the ball into zone 2 (the penalty area) and finish. See figure 13.25.

Special rule

In zone 2 the finish is made after a maximum of two touches.

Variations

1. One of the defenders may run into zone 2.
2. The ball may be passed into zone 2.
3. The attackers have a maximum of two touches.

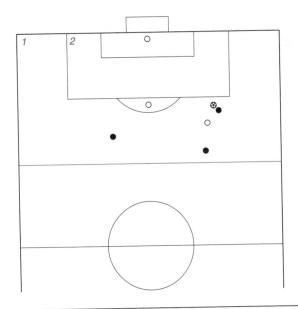

Figure 13.25 Change of tempo.

Hints for instruction

The exercise familiarizes the players with the transition from combination play to breakthrough. It focuses on the breakthrough player's change of tempo.

In variation 1 the players must evaluate when it is appropriate to set a breakthrough going. Variation 2 emphasizes the need for a pass forward into zone 2 to a breakthrough player. Variation 3 increases the need for the players to orient themselves and assess breakthrough opportunities.

This drill can also be used to introduce the situation where a player is in a 1-v-1 against the goalkeeper (see page 192), by replacing the special rule with the condition that finishing in zone 2 takes place within 10 seconds.

Keywords

Breakthrough player: change of tempo, assessment

Other members of the team: create space, offer oneself

About the Authors

Jens Bangsbo has been playing and coaching soccer for more than 35 years. He spent 15 years as a top-level player in Denmark, playing more than 400 matches in the top Danish league. In international play, he represented Denmark as both a youth player and as a member of the "A" national team. He is the advisor to the Danish national teams and assistant head coach to the Italian league's Juventus FC. An instructor at the Danish Football Association since 1986, Bangsbo has published more than 100 articles on soccer and conditioning. He also has written several books, including *Soccer Systems & Strategies* and *Defensive Soccer Tactics* together with Birger Peitersen.

Birger Peitersen is also one of Denmark's top soccer figures, having coached the Danish women's national team and the national champions of the men's league and serving as staff coach of the Danish Football Federation. In 1982, he received the highest coaching award in Denmark, the Diploma in Elite Soccer Coaching. Peitersen was the expert commentator for international European matches on Danish television in the UEFA Champions League and for Danish radio at the World Cup in 1990, 1998, and 2002 and the European Championships in 1992, 1996, and 2000.

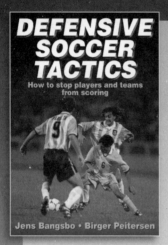
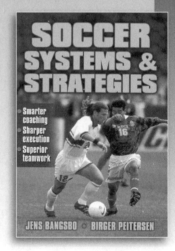